STOIC ASCENT

RAHAIL KHAN

First published 2023
by Rowanvale Books Ltd
The Gate
Keppoch Street
Roath
Cardiff
CF24 3JW
www.rowanvalebooks.com

A CIP catalogue record for this book is available from the British Library.

ISBN: 978-1-914422-56-0
Hardback ISBN: 978-1-914422-57-7
eBook ISBN: 978-1-914422-55-3

Acknowledgements

First of all, I am thankful to have come across this wisdom, which has enabled me to progress along my journey and become able to share this wisdom with the readers of this book.

I am thankful to the adversities I have faced, through which I was able to build my character.

To my close ones in my inner circle: you are few, and you know who you are. I thank you for standing by me through my journey to the present.

To those who have presented themselves as part of my adversities, I thank you as well. You have provided me with many opportunities to utilise the lessons from the Stoics whilst remaining true to my heart.

I am thankful to the readers of this book, for we are together on this journey of living in accordance with nature.

Contents

Images

Introduction
Why Choose the Stoic Path?

The aim of this book is to introduce you to the concepts of Stoicism and show you how they can be used to build one's character. Throughout the book, we will explore what the Stoic ideal of a good man is and how we can become that. I consider the wisdom of the Stoics to be a continuation of the wisdom our parents imparted to us along our journey towards adulthood, although the depth of wisdom found within the Stoic outlook is something all can benefit from.

This is not intended as an academic study of Stoicism—we are only seeking to gain insight from it for practical benefits. Once we become familiar with these concepts, then we shall see how we can apply such wisdom to our own lives.

There is a misunderstanding in the modern world that Stoicism is a passive outlook, but if you follow the Stoic path of this book, you will find yourself equipped with a powerful psychology that will assist you with overcoming any adversity, whether you are confronting it in the realm of the inner self or the external world. It is my aim to equip you with all the tools and concepts of the Stoics, thus allowing you to discern with your highest potential of rationality whether to take an active or inactive approach when faced with a particular adversity. Whichever choice you make, you will have based it on the underlying reasoning of the Stoic principles. With these tools and concepts, you can rise to new heights that were once unknown.

The Stoics were master logicians and understood clearly how to avoid matters that would take them off the path, which they considered the highest good. In the modern age of information overload, these Stoic methods to prevent us from being diverted off our paths can benefit us greatly. These skills are needed even more so now than in ancient times.

Once you have mastered the concepts presented in this book, you are, for the most part, less likely to suffer from mental health issues. The Stoics were regarded as the psychologists of ancient times, and by following their teachings, I have personally benefitted by overcoming certain adversities of this kind. Much of this we can achieve just by understanding the two realms of the inner self and the external world. At the moment, you operate in the external world with your existing level of wisdom, accumulated from your learning and experiences. In this book, I will present to you a new way of seeing things as they are so that you can become the master of yourself.

This book is a good starting point for those who are new to philosophy and have, for whatever reason, decided to approach this subject and see for themselves just how much this time-tested philosophy can assist if it becomes part of a person's outlook. This book can be of much benefit for such people to explore the Stoic path, which is a far more practical philosophy than most other schools of thought.

Stoicism is not about fluff and is concise in how its ideas are presented, leaving little room for various interpretations. In the following chapters, I will also explore deeper concepts of Stoicism, but these concepts will be presented in such a way that you can also apply them to your life should a situation present itself that can only be resolved through understanding such concepts.

This book can be part of your journey of self-discovery. As we traverse this path, you will learn many aspects of it and see how they can relate to you. Some concepts may not resonate with you immediately, but contemplating them may serve as a springboard to a different way of thinking, in which they start to make sense. This is yet another aim of this book: I'm not going to tell you what to think, but rather *how* to think. With this kind of methodology, you will acquire wisdom for yourself. You will ascend through these ideas, following each to its logical conclusion for you. This is why the book is called *Stoic Ascent*.

I also welcome you to enjoy a wealth of resources on our website stoicascent.co.uk and our YouTube channel, to which insightful Stoic videos are added on a weekly basis.

There is a quote by Marcus Aurelius: "Run always the short road, and Nature's road is short. Therefore say and do everything in the soundest way."

I hope every reader of this book will start their journey while keeping in mind the outlook of this quote. As, hopefully, I will be a useful guide to a certain point, but there are always higher mountains to ascend, and you will continue your journey alone once you are done here. Perhaps, we shall meet again at a yet higher point and see the view from there.

"Repeatedly dwell on the swiftness of the passage and departure of things that are of things that come to be. For substance is like a river in perpetual flux. Its activities are in continuous changes, and its causes are in myriad varieties, and there is scarce anything which stands still, even if near at hand; dwell too on the infinite gulf of the past and the future."

—Marcus Aurelius

The ethics of Stoicism have a solid grounding based on justice, temperance, courage and wisdom. All people can resonate with these qualities, which are universally recognisable. We could all pay more attention to these qualities, though, which would bring forth a vast number of benefits.

As the passage of life is so swift, our focus should be on bringing forth change for the better to the external world, but this can only be possible after the same has been carried out within one's inner world. One must learn to control their own emotions, not to eradicate them but rather to domesticate them. This allows for a clarity of thought, thus enabling one to deal with any situation more correctly.

"Do not act unwillingly nor selfishly nor without self-examination, nor with divergent motives. Let no affectation veneer your thinking. Be neither a busy talker nor a busybody."
—Marcus Aurelius

Stoicism is a philosophical school of thought that dates back to Zeno of Citium from Athens. One of the most notable Stoic thinkers of later times is Marcus Aurelius, the emperor of Rome during an era when the Roman Empire was at its height of power. The earliest full writings we have on Stoic philosophy are from Seneca, Epictetus and Marcus Aurelius. Within them, we find demonstrations of propositional logic and a focus on living in accordance with nature and being content with what one has in the present moment, thus enabling one to have greater self-control by not reacting to the external world, but instead enhancing one's internal faculties to judge any situation accordingly.

All individuals going through the journey of life will face adversity in one form or another. Whichever industry one works in, the higher one climbs the ladder of responsibility, the greater the challenges become. These challenges can be in the form of the skills needed, the situations faced, and the other people encountered, whether friends, family, associates or even humanity as a whole. Up against such obstacles, how will you make the best decisions and take the right actions? From what place will you find your north star of guidance, and what will keep you grounded? And how will you build your character to become the sort of person who knows how to make these changes?

The modern world presents challenges quite different from the ancient world, but the Stoic path can certainly provide the answers to these questions, both in regard to our inner selves and the external world we find ourselves in. Here in this book, you will find the ideas of the Stoic philosophers, which many in the modern world have not been introduced to. Even if you are familiar with the Stoics, then exactly how to apply their ideas in these modern times might have eluded you. Though times may be tough, remember that it is in our darkest hour that the spark of genius appears, if we know where to look.

Equanimity, or psychological stability, is much sought after by the Stoic, who seeks to be unmoved by forces from both the external world and from within. From the internal world, these forces can be emotions or incorrect thoughts. The external forces are caused by situations and other people that are not aligned with the Stoic's beliefs and attitude in any particular moment.

The Stoics believed in thinking in the present moment, which can create a more focused ability to actually live in the moment by not worrying about the past or the future. Living in accordance with nature is also mentioned throughout the Stoic writings, which can be seen as both the nature of the world, as in the natural order of things, and human nature. Human nature is a broad term, although as the Stoics understood it, it referred to all that is intrinsically and innately good from a human standpoint. Another meaning of "living in accordance with nature" is to follow the nature of the universe and reject self-tyranny. Intrinsic genuine moral value, duty, rationale and choice are all part of living in accordance with nature, as are the reason and superiority that lift us from the brute. From this, all morals of impropriety are derived, and upon it depends the rational method of ascertaining our duty.

The outlook of the Stoics therefore looks to build our wisdom, which is part of the world of the inner self, to new heights. This undertaking can be more easily progressed as one learns to domesticate one's emotions and be unaffected by them.

The following chapters will discuss the concepts of Stoicism to demonstrate their effectiveness in building one's character from the ground up. Other concepts will present a way of looking at the external world and provide a Stoic path to traverse towards self-discovery. You will then see that any challenges you face can be dealt with accordingly using the Stoic principles.

There are four principles of Stoicism: self-discipline, justice, courage and wisdom, which together lead towards the concept of virtue. Mastering these principles is like learning anything else in life: you must direct your focus towards attaining such things, and in doing so, wisdom shall be gained. You become the sculptor and the marble; the true character shall appear, who is the master of these four principles. While on your journey, you may look foolish to those around you, or seem like you are changing. This may fill you with anxiety, but with an understanding of Stoic concepts, we can learn how to separate the cause, which is part of the external world, from the effect it has in our internal world. Once this has been carried out correctly, the wisdom of how to control that which is within our power accordingly presents itself.

So, you are in the boardroom or a team meeting and all those present believe in doing things differently from you. Many opinions are being thrown around, and there seems to be no agreement with you in particular; you are not being listened to properly. How does one of high character and wisdom deal with such a situation? Do you walk out? Do you let the team proceed, even though you see gaps in their logic? Do you go with the flow, although your duty is for the betterment of the organisation? Of course, this example is within a professional context and might not be relevant to everyone, but the key thing to see is the conflict arising between the inner world and the external world. Stoic philosophy covers both realms, and you can apply its teachings in this or any other setting you can think of. It is the intention of this book to have already done the heavy lifting and now present to you a Stoic journey which, if understood and applied, shall provide you with an arsenal of tools to overcome any adversity the modern world has to present.

We shall here start the journey towards becoming a sage, one who is always able to see the truth, as the Stoics tried to become themselves. Reaching this position will certainly take mastering all the concepts the Stoics have imparted to us. The four principles of this philosophy are the foundation upon which we will build our character from the ground up.

Within the following chapters, you will see how to use critical thinking from first principles to increase problem-solving skills, as well as Stoic concepts such as logic, predication, epistemology, metaphysics and ontology. Our focus will always remain on the practical application of these ideas, not the academic realms.

As useful as our emotions are, we shall learn to domesticate them accordingly through training so they do not rule us. Through sufficient self-discipline, you can avoid getting angered—but how? The Stoics noted that the one who angers you is then able to control you. Being grounded in logic allows you to swiftly see what needs to be seen as it should be and not as what we wish it to be. In the fast-paced information age of the modern world, this is particularly important, even more so than it was in the ancient times.

Those who start their journey along the Stoic path will soon learn what is needed to gain back control of themselves, for it seems this, to some extent, might have been eroded in the age of social media, where we are presented only with conclusions and not the foundations upon which these conclusions were built. It might be prudent for us to equip ourselves with the very same tools the philosophers used to deal with such things. Later, we'll see in detail how we can incorporate these tools into our lives to enable us to overcome any adversity in a wide spectrum of things.

As the concepts of Stoicism start to become second nature to you, you will start to embody this philosophy and develop skills that many are lacking in the present day, such as thinking on your feet. You won't just be giving quick, unsound answers, but you'll be able to answer with knowledge, reaching a kind of flow state of mind.

In the modern world, there appears to be a lack of consistency from many people. They do not appear to have a clear set of principles they are guided by. To achieve a more consistent worldview and set of behaviours, one should focus on what is within their control and find a set of principles that they believe in. Looking at things from different angles can help us to gain insight, but what we see will depend on the principles we hold. As we too are part of the modern world, then with the use of Stoic philosophy we can find a way to remain consistent in our philosophical standpoints, then see where else in our lives there is inconsistency. Inconsistency can arise from people holding a position and then becoming led by emotion and biases, which we all have. The Stoics were very much aware of biases and attempted to deal with them so they did not influence their thinking. Our internal biases, like many other aspects, will be discussed throughout the following chapters.

I will mention here that I come from an Islamic background. In fact, it is one of the very things that drew me to the Stoic path. The way in which the character should be built in Stoicism is similar in many regards to the way Islam describes. I will also note here that it is my belief that Islam is completely true and nothing else is needed to substitute it. As I became aware of and applied the concept of the Stoic epistemology in this regard, I continued to hold this opinion. If you're not inclined towards any religious affiliations, don't worry—this is not at all a book about comparing and combing religion and Stoicism. I simply had to get this point out there, as I know that when others from my background come across this, they might ask about such a thing. Now that I have covered this, we can continue this worthy journey.

"Be courageous without overstepping this quality as you will be seen as a brute and easily fall into the trappings of those astute of knowing how to deal with the likes of these type of men."

—Epictetus

This might be something to consider. It is worth pointing out that this quote is referring to being even-minded in this regard; you should avoid being a brute but still remain courageous.

Mastering ourselves is certainly important, and the Stoics' time-tested methodology for achieving this will be discussed in much detail in later chapters.

Here is a good time to mention that virtue is considered the highest good in the Stoic school of thought. It has been mentioned by these thinkers that even-mindedness is the greatest of qualities we can possess. Thus, as we progress through these chapters, we shall become more aware of how to apply this concept to any situation.

We will see that the workings of the inner self are the first thing that the Stoic should master. This controls our conduct towards others, as well as, more broadly, the ways in which we operate within the external world. To continue towards virtue, one must make progress in both realms. Virtue covers a vast spectrum of things that will provide a greater freedom in particular as there are many shackles that hold us down. It is noted by the Stoics that only the educated are free, whether this be from the inner realm or the external world.

It is important to maintain an even-minded approach towards the Stoic school of thought. We should take from it what is most beneficial to us and acknowledge that not every aspect will be applicable for every individual. Even if there are some aspects of the lives or personal actions of the Stoics that are not to our liking, we should not be concerned with this, as these matters did not influence their teachings from which we should take wisdom. However, we should not take the Stoic philosophy as God's word—or that of the ancient Greek gods, who would've been more familiar to the Stoics.

I would here refer back to the concept of being aligned with that which is spiritually superior as is covered in another chapter in more detail. If anyone studying the epistemology of the Stoics arrives at the conclusion that there must be a first cause, a designer with intelligence, then it would be logical for them to look into the monotheist beliefs that are still present within the modern world. After all, the Stoics, despite their great wisdom, were mere mortals finding their ways for themselves and helping those on the same path.

In recent years, we have seen a growing interest in the Stoic school of thought. This re-emergence could be due to the fact that the very aspects that this school provides have been eroding away within the modern world. People are looking for some level of grounding to keep themselves steady in a fast-paced world of constantly-evolving ideas that have not yet stood the test of time.

In this age of instant fame and riches, many young people do not realise what is truly required to become successful.

They have attained fame and riches without ever overcoming adversity or building their character. They have missed out on so much that they are not aware of. And though such instant success is only the reality for a lucky few, the rest expect the same easy progression through life. All of the building of character, the seeking and attaining wisdom, the ethics and principles that provide the betterment of the inner self and the external world along the Stoic path are lost in the process. When was the last time we heard the term "virtue" in the media? I myself cannot recall such a mention, let alone hearing the details of what it entails. I recently asked many people when they last heard the word "virtue" and to define what it means to them. All answered that they did not recall hearing it, and they all struggled to define the word. However, many recalled this modern thing called "virtue signalling", which is the opposite of virtue as the Stoics understood it. This poses a question: how is it possible for people to pursue virtue when they do not know what it is?

In this book, I wish to bring to your attention the very best of what Stoicism has to offer and show you how to utilise it.

"If anyone tells you that a certain person speaks ill of you, do not make excuses about what is said of you but answer, 'He was ignorant of my other faults, else he would not have mentioned these alone.'"
—Epictetus

This quote provides one such example of the many things that were discussed by Stoic philosophers and are still relevant today, as many in our times regard what others say perhaps more than they value their own opinions. The Stoic path might be the path that leads to becoming a psychological warrior who can navigate within the storm rather than waiting for it to pass. Be in pursuit of courage by knowing what is the right thing to do, and have the self-discipline to stay on the path. In the modern world, the Stoic concepts can be elusive and almost invisible. Hence, we must keep this principle of self-discipline in mind for it will be required along this journey, which if taken with an even mind will lead us to heights previously not seen.

"From this instant on, vow to stop disappointing yourself. Separate yourself from the mob. Decide to be extraordinary and do what you need to—now."

—Epictetus

The further you go along the path, the wiser you will find yourself becoming.

Wisdom is to be sought along the Stoic path, yet what does it mean to be wise? To be wise is to have gone through many situations and experienced the highs and lows of life, to have learned from the education of moment after moment. Everyone attains this to some extent, although we are directed by the Stoics to seek this knowledge more swiftly.

The principle which is at the peak of Stoicism is virtue. But what is virtue and what does it consist of? There will be differences of opinion in this regard, but I shall attempt to simplify this. Virtue is a combination of the first four principles of Stoicism—wisdom, courage, temperance and justice, all of which we shall explore further in later chapters. A person of true virtue is modest in their approach to it, and it is so that they become a person who has attained virtue. A person of little virtue, on the other hand, strives to attain virtue, and so it is that they become a person whom virtue has eluded.

By practising these virtuous qualities daily, you will move further towards looking within yourself and to the external world with more depth and clarity. You will well be on your way down the Stoic path, which is not a well-trodden path in our times. The footprints that were once easily visible are now quite faded, yet those who are seeking this path still have a chance of pursuit.

Lessons From Leaders
Who Used Philosophy

Those who are not familiar with Stoic philosophy may think that it is only an undertaking by old men in robes, sitting around in their leisurely lives. There may be some truth to this stereotype when it comes to philosophy in general, but the Stoics did not pursue philosophy for purely academic purposes. By standing on the shoulders of these giants, we can gain a deeper understanding of ourselves and the external world. Some of us may have a great number of life experiences that will have served us well, others may not, but either way all of us can benefit from reading about those who dedicated their lives to seeking to pursue their philosophy.

Personally, I never came across any philosophical works in my early years, and pretty much thought of the entire subject as something very complex and of not much practical use. I realised I was quite wrong in my thinking when I came across the works of Marcus Aurelius and started to understand the gems of wisdom and practical advice within. I started putting them into practice for myself and benefitting from them on a regular basis. My discovery was just amazingly well timed, as it was exactly what I needed at that stage of my self-development. Stoicism opened up new paths to success that were different from those suggested in the business and self-development books I had looked into before coming across the Stoic path.

Looking towards the likes of Marcus Aurelius and Seneca, who held high positions of power and adopted the Stoic way of thinking, can show us that there is much wisdom to be found in such a philosophy. What are the elements of Stoicism that would have benefitted those in such positions? Well, any situation we face in reality can be misjudged, even by the most astute of those who possess wisdom. In the following chapters, we will explore how combining a number of Stoic concepts can help improve one's ability to make quick decisions. Our emotional states can often hinder our ability to make sound decisions, as they can make us incorrectly comprehend events and oversee details. By domesticating our emotions according to the Stoic concepts of passions and impressions, we will be able to avoid such pitfalls.

In Stoic philosophy, the present moment holds the greatest importance. The past and future are secondary by their nature, as the present is always with us and is truly the only thing that one really owns. Grounding oneself in the present can help in attaining a tactical and strategic position with wisdom. By recognising the past and future as separate from the present, one can avoid having their judgement clouded by past impressions and opinions, thus allowing one to fully appreciate the now. This clarity of perception towards the external world will then assist in simplifying the Stoic path onward towards virtue.

"Some things are hastening to be, others to have come and gone, and a part of what is coming into being is already extinct. Flux and change renew the world incessantly, as the unbroken passage of time makes boundless eternity ever young. In this river, therefore, on which he cannot stand, which of these things that race past him should a man greatly prize? As though he should begin to set his heart on one of the little sparrows that fly past, when already it has gone away out of his sight."

—Marcus Aurelius

Stoicism emphasises that the pursuit of material possessions should not be the highest aim one should have. This philosophy is relevant in the modern world, even more so than it was in ancient times. As the world is in constant change, we must align ourselves with nature in order to maintain a constant flow towards virtue. However, it is a misconception that Stoicism advocates a complete lack of want for material things and a passive reaction to the world. Rather, the philosophy can be applied in a broader sense, encompassing both the internal aspects of oneself and the external world. As long as we keep in mind the importance of living in accordance with nature and virtue, and do not allow these to become secondary priorities, then there is no harm in seeking possession of material things.

Marcus Aurelius, who was emperor of Rome, applied the Stoic philosophy and led the empire, even through some turbulent times. This is evident in his work, the *Meditations*, which were actually his personal notes. This makes it clear that Stoicism does not advocate a monk-like lifestyle, but rather takes the position that one should very much be part of society. By focusing on excellence in their pursuits, they can bring themselves towards virtue as the highest goal.

If the pursuit of virtue is forgotten, then we ultimately get the modern ways of thinking, which are more ideological than religious or philosophical. Adopting the philosophical principles of the Stoics will bring similar kinds of benefits to those mentioned by Sun Tzu in *The Art of War*: "Know thyself and know thy enemy. A thousand battles, a thousand victories." Although the Stoic path is not focused on actual battles in the same way as Sun Tzu's works, we can see similarities between the two. The Stoics focused on the betterment of building one's character and living in accordance with nature, which in this regard refers to living in complete rationality. This path certainly provides the methods to attain such a life.

The journey of life that all people must travel through is about overcoming adversity. Then the question arises: should we equip ourselves with the concepts and tools of the philosophers to gain an advantage on this journey, when we are presented with so many ideas and information from different sources as to how and what we should be? In this book, I intend to show you that anyone will be better placed to deal with life's adversities when equipped with these Stoic tools. The Stoic knows that there is always a space between action and reaction where they can choose what to do next. Even though this space can be narrow, the Stoic tools of logic and reason can help us to make decisions quickly and deal with any situation accordingly. As you progress towards the horizon of the Stoic path, you will indeed bring forth a formidable character from within yourself.

Everyone who reads this book will approach it from a unique perspective, as each person's situation and context will be different from each other at the time of reading. Some readers may adopt some of these new concepts in order to overcome particular challenges they are facing. Some will remove or rethink their current ways of thinking, which they will realise are no longer serving them as well as they once did. Some will become enlightened in a more general way, acquiring new wisdom. This includes myself, as we are on a journey together on this path, and I welcome all those who are here with strength and honour.

Amor fati, a Stoic principle we will discuss further later, refers to the concept of loving fate. Perhaps it is fate that has brought you here to read this wisdom, which will provide you with the tools to make a better fate for yourself. At first glance, *amor fati* may be understood as simply accepting anything that happens and adopting a passive approach to life. This is a misunderstanding of the principle. Rather, it involves first looking at the external world and understanding it for what it really is. Then, to look within and better understand ourselves using the Stoic principles. Then, finally, we may look again at the external world and bring about a change therein for the better.

"He who loves glory thinks the activity of another to be his own good; he who loves pleasure thinks his own feeling to be his good; he who has intelligence thinks his own action to be good. It is possible to entertain no thought about this, and not to be troubled in spirit; for things of themselves are not so constituted as to create our judgements upon them."

—Marcus Aurelius

By knowing yourself, you will be better equipped to find wisdom that takes some work to attain. This can be achieved by applying the concepts presented throughout this book. Learning who you truly are is certainly a worthy task, as if you try to become someone else then at best you will only become a reflection of that person. This is particularly important in the modern world, as there are fewer role models of good and high character. Ultimately, the purpose of this book is to enable you to carry out the work of self-development for yourself by applying the concepts of Stoic philosophy to your internal self and the external world.

How, then, do you get to know yourself? Could it be that you are ignorant about yourself? Well, you can start by asking yourself the right questions to give you a greater insight into yourself. Here are some suggestions:

Some questions to assist on your Stoic Journey

1. When I think of myself by looking within, am I humble enough to see the truth of what I am, or do I tell myself a story about who I want to be?

2. What makes me tick and motivates me?

3. What makes me procrastinate and demotivates me?

4. What are my core beliefs that ground my thoughts?

5. Over the last six months, what has held me back, and what obstacles have I overcome to progress towards where I want to be?

6. Have I thought through my core beliefs with reasoning, logic and rationality?

7. Have the opinions I hold been formulated by myself, or have they been given to me by my peers?

8. Am I afraid of making mistakes because of what others say?

9. Am I fine with making mistakes along the way towards my goals?

10. After reading this book, how much will I contemplate and take action on the wisdom therein?

Discipline is crucial for making progress with any endeavour, and this is true for the Stoic path, for there will be various challenges ahead. While one may choose not to adopt voluntary hardships like the Stoics did, some of the self-imposed pressure of these principles may be beneficial. Seneca suggests we ask ourselves: "What obstacles did I overcome today and what virtues did I attain today?" This can serve as a good starting point to fan the flames of your spirit so that they may burn brighter and help you in pursuit of your goals along this path, which are in agreement with nature. Once you see that which only you can see, then you have the courage for such a pursuit.

This brings our attention to the resistance we may face from various external sources. It's normal to face such challenges. A person can only be seen as virtuous after overcoming adversity. When faced with obstacles in any pursuit, it is best to think of them as plateaus rather than limits. Practising applying Stoic concepts in small steps daily, as required, will certainly bring forth the desired results.

Another notable example of a leader who followed the Stoic philosophy was Hadrian, the Roman emperor who most notably built Hadrian's Wall, a Roman fortification that still stands today. Most of Hadrian's military activities were driven by his ideology of empire and community of mutual interest, which focused more on dealing with internal and external threats than the expansion of the empire.

Concepts of Competitiveness Within Stoicism

It is well known that the ancient Stoic thinkers valued moderation. This mindset encourages individuals to avoid extremes in any regard. However, there are exceptions to this. For example, no Stoic would apply the concept of moderation to a sound pursuit that aligns with Stoic values, such as the pursuit of virtue. Thus, if we have found a pursuit that is for the betterment of ourselves or the external world then we may not need to apply this concept in its fullest sense. In fact, we may instead need to apply all that we can to that endeavour, whether it be in sports, business or anything else.

The practice of self-imposed hardship, which we can see in how young Marcus Aurelius slept on the hard floor despite being next in line to become Caesar of Rome, was a method used by the Stoics to prepare the mind for adversity. This was a common practice among the Stoics, but they did not subject themselves to it constantly, instead using the practice in particular circumstances to help them achieve increased mental toughness, fortitude, resilience and to separate themselves in the short term from material possessions and comforts. They may have utilised this practice to test their endurance and discipline. Through this, they would be better equipped to tackle any external adversity that came their way with greater ease, as they had already been battle-tested within their minds. It is a wise man's task to discern the ideal intensity and frequency of this kind of practice.

Being prudent, we should take the best that Stoicism has to offer based on our individual circumstances and situations, perhaps not embracing every concept to its fullest extent. By doing this, we're actually applying the concept of being even-minded, which the Stoics say is the greatest virtue. Just remember not to hold conflicting views simultaneously, as this can lead to faults within our logic. For example, certainly not all of us want to completely stay away from the finer things that the external world has to offer, as long as they do not become the only or main focus in our lives. The pursuit of good quality things is not inherently harmful; it is our attitude towards this that matters.

The question arises as to whether Stoic practitioners of this kind of mental conditioning believe in the concept of competition. It is easy to fall into the trap of believing the Stoics were completely passive or monk–like, when in fact, being competitive whilst remaining with a Stoic outlook is very possible. In the first instance, the Stoics competed with themselves, and with competing schools of thought, with which the Stoics engaged in many discourses. It can be said that the Stoics were in competition with themselves as they furthered themselves towards virtue and with regard to becoming a sage. The effectiveness of this is clear from the fact that many prominent Stoic teachers, unlike most others in competing schools of thought, held high positions of responsibility within Roman society.

Stoic literature, discourses and letters position the reader as a student and the Stoic as the teacher. Without a general Stoic society at play in our times, we do not get an insight into how there would have been competition between the thinkers, as we do not visibly see the Stoics outdoing each other in applying the principles and reaching for virtue.

The modern world, with its focus on careers and business, is inherently competitive. If we do not have a competitive outlook, we can quite easily fall behind and remain in places where we do not desire to be. So, we should make sure we have a little sense of urgency when travelling the Stoic path, for—as the Stoics have often mentioned—life is short. Every time we fall, we should get right back up with resilience, fortitude and mental toughness. To do so is to compete with ourselves, as we make sure not to let adversity slow us down but instead gain wisdom from it. By embodying these Stoic qualities, you will put yourself ahead of the curve of competition, who lack such resilience. You will have made yourself more focused and sharper, able to solve problems and overcome adversity.

Marcus Aurelius was known as the "last of the five good emperors", the others being his predecessors—Nerva, Trajan, Hadrian and Antonio Pius. These five were more focused on bringing about stability within the Roman Empire than the expansion of territory. I would include here an example from the lives of Hadrian and Marcus Aurelius to show how particular aspects of Stoicism can be applied in the face of adversity, such as that faced on the battlefield, but the relevant stories are very short and their details limited.

While there are vast numbers of short stories, letters and quotes available throughout Stoic literature, there are few detailed narratives of the journeys and experiences of these characters for us to draw upon. As I could not find a suitable tale of one of the ancient Stoics, I considered including a story from another source and viewing it through a Stoic lens. Although this could have been an interesting exercise to carry out, I was pretty certain that more advanced Stoic readers would have seen this as superimposing Stoicism where it does not necessarily apply. However, for those interested in a great tale from history that could be seen as showing the competitive mindset being applied from a Stoic point of view, I would read *The Sultan's Admiral* by Ernle Bradford, which tells the swashbuckling story of Barbarossa.

In the pursuit of such examples, we should ask what such characters would look like in our modern world today. It may very well be those who undertake the Stoic journey for themselves who become the examples we are looking for. If we were to find a character such as Marcus Aurelius here in our times, we would see how he applied the Stoic concepts we have mentioned throughout this book to the various endeavours that we pursue in our businesses and careers. Though you might not be aiming directly to become a sage, a Stoic concept referring to one who is always able to see the truth, to some extent just traversing the Stoic path will lead you in this direction anyhow. Therefore, if there are no modern heroes to look up to, we have in front us a clear framework with which we can create this very thing and become our own heroes.

Let's return our attention to the concept of moderation and being content with what we already have. How do we reconcile this with responsibilities we may have, such as being answerable to business stakeholders or managers at work who have tasked us with increasing revenue? Or, in our personal lives, the desire to progress in our careers as we seek to provide a better quality of life for ourselves and our families? I would argue that the best way to reconcile these goals with a moderation-focused outlook would be to focus on being grateful for what we have in our possession at any given time. Once we have internalised this and ordered our minds, we will have found balance in the inner self, and can then focus on the external world to bring about positive change. If you are employed within a business and are accountable to managers or stakeholders, you should work towards the betterment of the business, as otherwise your presence within it will hinder it to some extent. The same applies to the betterment of ourselves and our families.

"It is amid stumblings of this sort that you must travel out this rugged journey. Does one wish to die? Let the mind be prepared to meet everything; let it know that it has reached the heights round which the thunder plays. Let it know that it has arrived where —
Grief and avenging Care have set their couch,
And pallid sickness dwells, and drear Old Age.
With such messmates must you spend your days. Avoid them you cannot, but despise them you can. And you will despise them, if you often take thought and anticipate the future. Everyone approaches courageously a danger which he has prepared himself to meet long before, and withstands even hardships if he has previously practised how to meet them. But, contrariwise, the unprepared are panic-stricken even at the most trifling things. We must see to it that nothing shall come upon us unforeseen. And since things are all the more serious when they are unfamiliar, continual reflection will give you the power, no matter what the evil may be, not to play the unschooled boy."

—Seneca

Let's look at this excerpt from a letter by Seneca to find some insight regarding how a person in the modern world, equipped with the tools the Stoics have imparted, may demonstrate the Stoic mindset. We can gain insight from Seneca as we face our own challenging terrain. These Stoic concepts are just as relevant today as they were in the ancient world and can be applied universally to whichever endeavour you have chosen to pursue.

As you progress towards mastery in the external world, simultaneously you should work towards the mastery of the inner world through learning and applying Stoic principles with a focus towards virtue. Balancing these two worlds will in itself be a kind of adversity to overcome. However, those seekers who persist and continue further along this path than others will attain the wisdom of a sage. This kind of character-building will most certainly further enhance your ability to handle adversity presented to us by the external world, especially within the business and professional world. The challenges a business faces at each stage of growth will require a different set of skills from its key members, who will develop and adapt to overcome these new forms of adversity. In the same way, as one travels further along the Stoic path, they will need to develop new skill sets. The same impulse that started us upon this trajectory—the desire to make use of the tools from the Stoics and apply them to overcome adversity—will provide us with the power to continue upon it.

I have had experience with organisations that are headed by people who see things as they wish them to be more than as they are. Within a business environment, this inability to see the complete picture will hinder both the organisation and the personal growth of its team members. It would be prudent, then, to steer clear of the influence of those stuck in such mindsets. The Stoics often advised to take care of the impressions we make of the external world, and within the company of such people, we will inevitably be guided the wrong way.

Those who are more well-travelled on the Stoic path can attempt to impart their logic and wisdom to others who are seeking such knowledge for themselves. When listeners quickly show resistance to such concepts, we can understand if trying to teach them is a worthy undertaking. Here, we can learn from the discourses of Stoic literature, which provide wisdom without depicting their students responding with counterarguments or disagreement. From this, we might then discern that the Stoics only presented their advice to those who were either willing or had the grounding to take such information in. In similar situations, we too should impart our knowledge with discretion and wisdom. Rather than wasting our time trying to change the minds of other people that are beyond our control, we should pursue more worthy causes, such as steering our overall organisations in line with Stoic principles.

This could be one of the reasons why the five good emperors took the approach they did towards managing the Roman Empire. Perhaps the Stoic influence present at the time they came into their positions influenced them. As with most things, many other factors contributed to this decision, but it is quite a coincidence that these five took the same approach—one that notably followed the Stoic outlook. A clear example of this approach would be the building of Hadrian's Wall, which marked the limits of Roman expansion. It can be difficult to find a tale from history that shows one of these characters intending an action and then pursuing it to the journey's end, as we would be looking for the mindset, the planning, the actions and the results all within one tale.

We must use the ancient Stoics to discern what a modern Stoic should look like, and, in particular, how they can thrive within a competitive world. The wisdom of the Stoics can provide a clear path for the beginner, demonstrating how the beginner can apply these concepts within areas of their own life. We become the model the modern Stoic has to aspire towards, and we must then compete with ourselves to traverse this path, as the Stoics would have advocated.

Others may have a different understanding of Stoicism—and they are welcome to do so—but the interpretation presented here is built upon sound foundations. Any other interpretation can lead to contradictions for the modern reader, who might then believe that Stoicism is more like the other philosophies: an academic pastime of the elite with a great deal of leisure time. If this kind of outlook is taken, then the intention of this book will be missed. The average person does not have the luxury of free time and wealth to focus solely on the academic pursuits of philosophy, and this may be one of the major factors why the masses tend to avoid philosophy in the first instance, especially in this fast-paced modern world. We tend to assign more value to things that are useful from the start of our journey and allow the beginner to see the potential rewards of taking such a path. Through this practical application of Stoicism, you will soon see the benefits. It will not take years of mastery before becoming useful.

Of course, there is plenty within this book to keep the more advanced person's interest. Each individual's journey will be personal to them, and the workings of the inner self are something that should be revisited often. As you teach you learn again—which is something I am experiencing through writing this book and imparting the wisdom I have attained. We really do have a proclivity to serve others, and this is my attempt at such an undertaking.

I would hope that all the readers of this book will attain much benefit from it. One thing is clear: you have spent your money for this and taken time out to go through your journey with me, for which I commend you. So, let's say to each other here: "strength and honour to us." As we discussed a few moments ago, the intention to help those who seek a higher level of understanding is something that comes from a good place and can be seen as an indication of looking upon the external world and trying to make a change for the better.

This is an example of how once you have looked within yourself and worked on the internal world, the next step is to look at the external world and then bring about change for the better. Once this is done, we can adopt a competitive mindset as well, as the Stoics advised us to be strict with ourselves and tolerant with others. How then do we do this? Well, we should adopt this competitive mindset towards our own Stoic journey. However, it is important that we carefully choose our audience for whatever kind of discourse it may be that we are engaging in. The wrong audience, even if well intentioned, can render our efforts useless.

Living within a competitive and fast-paced world requires a certain amount of discipline and fortitude to not be swayed from our path or slow down our development. The modern world will not slow down equally for us. This kind of fast-paced life requires information to be processed at a fast rate. This includes problem-solving and decision-making processes, which demand that we constantly confront varied and complex problems.

Under these circumstances and pressures, no matter what organisation you find yourself in, there will be an aspect of competition that you have to deal with. This may be in the form of actual competitors that are competing for market share, or the business landscapes and the economy. If we do not consider these things, it can severely hinder our progression or even the survival of our organisations.

In such an environment, it will serve us well to keep a level of discipline towards the course of our journey and to remember the direction we sought at its outset. As many a wise man has imparted to his audience, it is the way in which we look upon our work that will provide us with the motivation to keep going. Such motivation comes directly from doing that which we are passionate about. Motivation and passion are things that we have discussed in part in another chapter, but here too it is worth mentioning them, as it is easy to be swayed by emotion in such a state, so we must make sure to evaluate all positions and stances we take with logic and reason, to ensure our passions are aiding us rather than hindering us.

"I tell you all this just to show you the tremendous enthusiasm with which the merest beginner will set about attaining the very highest goals provided someone gives him the necessary prompting and encouragement."

—Seneca

Although the search for motivation to continue our journey may lead us to seek examples from the modern world, it is my intention here to bring our attention to ourselves, so that we may provide the necessary examples when we may not have others around us to fulfil this task. In any endeavour, all beginners have a keen motivation, but this motivation may not last the entire journey. It is exactly when we see that motivation suffer wear and tear along the way that most will turn back or towards another direction. At such a point, you shall need all the tools, as we have discussed thus far in this chapter, to take that next step needed to continue the journey. You must provide the example for your own success.

In the modern world, we are often presented with the idea that it is OK to prioritise comfort, which can make us soft in some regards and makes us remain in a comfortable condition quite opposite to the self-inflicted hardship of the Stoics.

We have not discussed competitiveness linearly but have explored the concept from a varied set of angles in the modern context. This ensures that we do not overlook anything that might prevent us from seeing the external world for what it really is.

The fact that particular people in the past who followed this school of thought were operating at the highest positions of office, such as Marcus Aurelius, further makes it clear that Stoicism is useful outside of academic realms. For example, much of Marcus Aurelius' *Meditations* was written whilst he was on campaigns. So, how would we place a character like this within the capitalistic business landscape that we find ourselves in today? What would their mode of operating be? How easily would they have been able to apply the Stoic principles to whatever they were doing? What we can say for sure is that applying Stoic principles would have been challenging in ancient times, just as it is in the modern world. Technological advancements do not mean anything in the realms of human nature and how we conduct ourselves with each other.

It should be mentioned here that the Stoic principles, as well as our path's direction towards virtue, should be internalised to build our character and the organisations we serve. Then why should we not compete in this manner as well, for the marketplace requires competition if we are to thrive within it? Likewise, competition was essential during the age of empires. No land had the option of simply staying out of the game of empire, when take or be taken was the norm.

Therefore, if we do not look at competition through a Stoic lens, we are committing the fallacy of not looking at the world for what it really is and instead wishing for it to be the way we want it to be. In various ways, we find ourselves under conditions in which we are forced to compete. But when there is no obvious opponent, who then are we to compete with? Well, then we should look within, and find a completely different realm of competition.

This was not a situation that the five good emperors ever found themselves in, as there was always external competition to be dealt with. They led the most powerful of all empires at the time; it was just a question of whether they would attempt to cross borders to expand their territories. For the most part, the threat of external invasion was not really a threat in their times. While we can still find insights in the works of these emperors and statesmen, it is unlikely that we will ever find ourselves in a parallel position of power.

Perhaps at those levels of power, we will only find individuals and organisations not willing to see the world for what it really is, who use their power to will the world to fit with how they want to see it. It would be wise for such people to instead grow their organisations steadily, and not push growth too far and spread themselves too thin.

With this wisdom, we can effectively ground our own journeys in sound principles that will provide us with the ethical groundwork to operate at a higher level in this regard. It is also true that honing your ability to truly see the external grants the ability to fully utilise analytical tools to solve problems of a more complex nature. A competitive or at least an ethical advantage may present itself from such insight.

Stoic principles emphasise the importance of being in accordance with nature. This alignment can act as a motivating force when the going gets difficult due to external pressure.

Mastery in any skill requires standing on the shoulders of giants, but we can only imagine the likes of Seneca advising us along this journey as we seek wisdom along our chosen paths. It raises the question as to whether we have enough from the Stoic teachers in their works that we have within our grasp to see us through the mud as we walk to higher ground. I would argue that we do. I say this due to my own personal growth I have experienced from applying the teachings of these great thinkers to my own life. There is value in taking wisdom from the Stoics and utilising that which is personally relevant to ourselves.

"If he exerts himself against them he will win. What in fact most people do is pull down on their own heads what they should be holding up against. When something is in imminent danger of falling on you, the pressure of it bearing heavily on you, it will only move after you and become an even greater weight to support if you back away from it; if instead you stand your ground, willing yourself to resist, it will be forced back."

—Seneca

Looking at such a statement from Seneca, we can gain insight into how to confront adversity and take appropriate action. When adversity presents itself, we are left with no option but to move forward. With a well-versed strategy and good tactics, all the tools we have picked up through wisdom, we can gain a competitive edge to overcome any adversity. This is one of the reasons I have chosen to focus on reconciling competition with the Stoic mindset, as this was often overlooked within Stoic literature. Whilst on this quest to attain mastery, we can tailor the nuances and finer details of Stoicism to meet our requirements for our personal use along the journey.

As we journey towards personal growth, it is crucial to remain even-minded whilst traversing the various kinds of terrain that are presented to us in both the inner and the external worlds. To make decisions wisely, we must therefore maintain an attitude of positive thinking, as we will discuss in another chapter. We should not be naive to what is going on around us, which may cause our impression of reality to be impaired in some way and lead us to fail to see the world for what it really is. Within the competitive landscape that we operate in, we should not compromise on the principles that we undertook so much work to embody in the first instance, even if it means competing at any cost to win. That being said, it is advisable to connect our thoughts to the aspects that we have discussed in the earlier chapter about emotions and human passions, and doing so will require discipline to build our character accordingly. Those who operate within this kind of landscape are far more likely to encounter aspects of themselves such as greed and dishonesty. The "ends justify the means" approach that is often found in such environments is not grounded at all within Stoic principles.

To keep moving forward, it is prudent to regularly recalibrate ourselves and acquire the skills needed to thrive within the environment in which we find ourselves. However, we must maintain an even-minded approach to achieve our desired targets, all the while attaining more wisdom as we progress to overcome every adversity that comes our way.

As you become more experienced, you will acquire greater wisdom, allowing the development of a holistic skillset that aligns with living in accordance with nature, allowing us to achieve new heights of our rationality. In addition, we must develop practical skillsets such as critical thinking to approach any adversity that presents itself.

The pursuit of even-mindedness can be challenging, particularly due to the fact that we are not attempting to remain in a passive, monk-like environment. Rather, within a competitive modern world, we are trying to break the barriers of both the inner and external realms, which in some ways enslave us. Once we understand how to apply Stoic thoughts to the world in which we find ourselves, we can unlock the full utility of these concepts. By internalising the very best of the wisdom Stoicism has imparted to us, we are able to face any situation, even one that the philosophy does not cover in its entirety, as we are still able to use our faculties to derive a way forward using what we have already learned. By seeing what concepts have helped us to progress and utilising these concepts, we can take the foresight and wisdom that is well within our grasp and use it to fill any gaps that may present themselves.

Every philosophy should be able to stand up to scrutiny based on logic and reasoning. We should not be easily swayed to take big leaps of faith without examining our motivations through such tests. The modern world at times demonstrates aspects that the Stoics would be quite averse to, such as motivations other than seeking the truth by way of virtue, ideas built on faulty premises and conclusions, and the unchecked presentation of inconsistencies. All of this is exacerbated by social media, which always seems to be flawed in one way or another, resulting in unchecked ideas that evolve at a rapid rate according to society's whims. Those who follow these trends in thinking seem to not be able to keep up with the rapid development of these ideas. Those upon the Stoic path instead have attained a level of wisdom separate from the trends of the day, and will not become distracted by such things, for part of the Stoic outlook is to become a sage and have the ability to always see the truth and the world for what it really is. In the early stages of my own Stoic journey, I found much of it resonated with me quite quickly, for the Islamic outlook also teaches to speak the truth even if it is against yourself.

Traversing the Stoic path will enable anyone to become more grounded with solid foundations that will help them avoid being overwhelmed by emotional reactions when faced with resistance. Rather, whenever such a thing presents itself, the Stoic is able to counter it swiftly with the use of logic and reasoning. As a result, it becomes harder to falter in the face of the modern world's challenges. This allows us to commit more time to working on ourselves and navigating the course towards virtue, as was the Stoics' aim.

We discussed in some detail how Stoic concepts can be applied to thrive in our modern competitive world. Now, I want to bring our attention to the competition between different philosophical schools of thought at the time of the Stoics, which still exists in some way today. Many of the Stoics' contentions were with the Epicureans, whose way of thinking seems quite the opposite of the Stoics' in many regards. There are many mentions of this discourse within the Stoic literature. In the modern world, this competition could be translated to the competing concepts of virtue and pleasure, or discipline and entertainment.

There are additional Stoic discourses that focus on the realm of philosophy itself, in which contentions are found with philosophers who either did not practise what they preached or made it a form of entertainment. Then also the philosophical schools of thought that were considered mere academic pastimes, which the Stoics found to be lacking in seriousness and practicality. We should take care not to be aimless in this way, as the Stoics advised.

We can understand from a modern perspective the likely reasons why Stoicism was left behind through the years. Through the process of competition, other philosophical schools became more popular. This could be attributed to the increased comfort and convenience available to the masses due to technological advancements, as well as the ideas of Enlightenment-era thinkers. Perhaps now we have taken these concepts a little too far, thus leading to the slow reemergence of Stoicism in recent times. It could be that we are realising that this kind of hyper-consumerism may not be the best thing for us. The increasing emphasis on being environmentally friendly might also have added to Stoicism gaining some momentum again, as living in accordance with nature is a central concept within this philosophy. In the background, Stoicism has been occupying a small yet growing space that has been leading people towards a more virtuous outlook, and often when people hear about this philosophy, they'll think to themselves: "This is what I was thinking anyway, and these guys have just articulated it."

We live in an era of super-fast information overload. The mass media and all kinds of other things demand our attention. With so many distractions, we need to be able to quickly discern what is truly worthy of our attention and direct our focus on more worthy things of higher importance. For the most part, these things are literally just background noise, which is easy to deal with. However, some of this information will still lead the masses in such a direction that may, if we follow this path, lead to a destination where no Stoics would ever arrive.

"When the object is not to make him want to learn but to get him learning, one must have recourse to these lower tones, which enter the mind more easily and stick in it. What is required is not a lot of words but effectual ones."

—Seneca

As students of Stoicism, we are the ones on the receiving end of such words. But do we always know who it is we sit in front of, and if their information comes from a sound place and has our best interests at heart? It would be prudent to remember that in such a scenario, a speaker may be manipulating their tone or using other forms of persuasion. We must not falter on the Stoic concepts we have discussed in this book, and remain steadfast along our path.

Let's return to the idea that with sound rationale, the Stoic teachings can perfectly be reconciled with seemingly contradictory ideas. We have here completely dispelled the misconception that the Stoics were passive and monk-like. Upon deeper reflection, we can come to the understanding that Stoic principles are very much compatible with the modern world that we find ourselves in. With the correct interpretation, we can use them to strengthen our character, attain wisdom and insight, and gain a competitive advantage, all the while never letting virtue leave our sights. When we find ourselves competing to further our careers and grow the organisations that we lead or serve, we can rest assured that by holding onto the Stoic principles, we have instilled these values within our character and promoted them to others within our organizations. By knowing this, we can be at peace to judge and act correctly, whatever the situation or adversity that presents itself to us.

Utilising our faculties to practise self-discipline by abstaining from over-indulgence and being grateful for the things we have been blessed with is certainly important. We should be able to recognise injustice no matter where we see it and act in such a way that leads us towards virtue as our guiding light—a light that never gets lost in the shadows. To be mindful of such things should be practised regularly. We must cultivate strength of character and know that wherever there is a human being, there is an opportunity for kindness. These Stoic practices are all things that will provide us with the tools we need to bring about the desired change within ourselves and the external world.

Whilst we are still discussing the subject within this chapter, we can view the external world as a form of competition between our current selves and our potential future selves. If competition is a thing that is inherently all around us, even from within ourselves, then why should we avoid it? By being aware of competition and accepting it, it can act as a motivating force that helps us to see a wider picture and places pressure on us to decide how to operate more effectively within such circumstances.

Choosing to embrace competition will surely lead us to a more advanced level on our Stoic journey. Our initial understanding of Stoic principles and the way in which we look upon the external world should be reevaluated in light of this new paradigm.

We all have the capability to look within ourselves and do the work as it should be done. It is worth knowing that this is not a well-worn path in the modern world. Along the way, you will encounter those who did not quite make it, and they should certainly be looked at as motivating factors. This is tied to the competitive aspects we were just discussing, as you strive to get further along this path than others. There is no need to stop to rest at these points even for a while, as there is nothing to contemplate—there is no wisdom at these points along the path. Instead, we should keep our sights upon the target that we set for ourselves before embarking on this journey, always knowing that something better lies ahead, and even if there is no end in sight, the pursuit should continue. The journey itself becomes the target, something quite worthy to be in pursuit of.

It is quite evident that positions of power come with competition and also with responsibility. It is important to be wise enough to see the world for what it is and to recognise that there will always be others who will want such a position for themselves. Many a Caesar has been killed for such reasons, as have those near him. The likes of Seneca and Marcus Aurelius were very well-versed in navigating these daily circumstances within such positions. Rather than merely surviving in these conditions, they were able to thrive.

When a stigma becomes attached to something, it can become difficult to remove. Unfortunately, the stigmas that are attached to Stoicism based on only surface-level understanding can give the impression to outsiders that Stoics are averse to possessing material things.

The Stoics intended to prepare the mind with the requisite mental toughness, resilience and fortitude for when adversity should present itself. Through such preparation, the Stoics were always ready to face such challenges. These practices should not be applied to our own lives literally but rather understood for their underlying insight and reasoning. We should learn from the wisdom of why such things were done by the Stoics and apply some parts of the same rigours to ourselves if we believe we would benefit from them.

Now we shall touch again upon the idea of competing with one's own self, for this very well can be of equal if not more importance than competition with others. The concepts we have discussed throughout this book, such as building character, instilling this philosophy's principles and being directed by virtue, are all related to the inner world of our being, and so as we seek to embody these concepts, we are effectively competing with ourselves. By conquering the self, we become free in the manner meant by the philosophers when they said that only the educated are free. Thus, this chapter is connected to the other parts of this book through the addition of this competitive mindset that will aid us in becoming freer than we were before and allowing us to look further towards the horizon.

For whatever reason, the masses are not free in the sense meant by Stoic teachers. To achieve this freedom through education, we must understand these concepts of building our character and instilling philosophical principles within ourselves. Only then can we take action to attain this true freedom, just as the philosophers did themselves.

In simple terms, we should compete with ourselves to progress towards achieving the reasoning that will provide us with the necessary skills to deal with whatever the external world presents to us, whether this be our own pursuits or adversity. We become aware of our own limitations and are better prepared to overcome any obstacles along our path.

"On such journeys you are prevented from going astray by some recognised road and by questions put to local people, but on this one all the most well-trodden and frequented paths prove the most deceptive. Accordingly, the most important point to stress is that we should not, like sheep, follow the herd of creatures in front of us, making our way where others go, not where we ought to go. And yet there is nothing that brings greater trouble on us than the fact that we conform to rumour, thinking that what has won widespread approval is best, and that, as we have so many to follow as good."

—Seneca

Each individual's path in regard to the inner self is unique, and uncharted territory, so you must walk it with the foresight to see past any deceptions as they arise. This is possible in two ways: firstly, by using the tools provided by the Stoic path; and secondly, through taking wisdom from the works of the Stoics. When we take a break from the path and look again to the external world to ask others for guidance, the advice we receive may be well-intentioned though based upon incomplete understanding, or it may even be deliberately deceptive. Therefore, the Stoics provided for themselves the analytical tools necessary to make decisions based on sound reasoning. They had the fortitude to remain upon those positions as needed, rather than fall into the continual reevaluating of ideas, as the Sceptics did.

It is important to note that in the modern world, we are not in the position of Hadrian, who could seek counsel directly from the Stoic teachers. Therefore, it is up to us to become fully capable of utilising Stoic philosophy to achieve our goals in the external world without being confused or distracted by external influences. In the modern world, we often see people following a certain path without looking into the details of it for themselves as they are simply following the herd. Only later do they realise that the herd was travelling in the wrong direction.

We can then take from this that the Stoics themselves quite possibly knew that their philosophy might well be the hardest to follow. Thus, it is reasonable to look within ourselves and question whether we have the mental toughness and resilience to continue along this path, as it will take continual intelligent action to remain upon it. Upon this path, we face the ultimate challenge of competing with ourselves to be better today than we were yesterday. Some days the terrain will be quite steady and other days it will be quite uneven, thus requiring different skills and adaptability to continue to traverse the path.

We must continue to build character with integrity, strength and honour, for these qualities are part of the pursuit of wisdom. Only those who actively seek such things shall truly attain them. One who seeks only what this external world has to offer might well attain such qualities, but the one who sought to develop these inner qualities will have built these attributes from within and gained more along the way, for this is in part living in accordance with nature itself.

Many people can innately recognise what is good, but developing this quality can require work and guidance from external sources. We encounter many things we see in our lifetimes, and without such guidance, we will be unable to see all of them from the correct point of view. Many aspects of our upbringing, location, experiences and societal pressures can keep us following our inherent inclination towards good. Therefore, training in this regard, along with education and character-building in ways that are aligned with our innate dispositions and nature, is essential. Such training will clear the mist from in front of us and reveal that there are actually two paths that we may follow: one that lets us forget our innate dispositions towards goodness, mental toughness and resilience; and one that we can only proceed upon if we simultaneously carry out the necessary work.

It can then be said that competition within a Stoic mindset is multifaceted, as we are competing with ourselves to build character, competing to live in accordance with nature, and competing with forces operating within the external world.

As we have demonstrated, if concepts of competition are used correctly, they can actually present us with an edge over those who do not use such concepts. We are free to operate wherever and with whomsoever we choose. As the Stoics advised us to live in accordance with nature, we can choose to operate within industries that align with such a concept, or we can choose to bring about betterment to the external world by pushing an industry in such a direction. We even can choose to start our own businesses with an outlook of being able to thrive in the marketplace along with keeping aligned with Stoic principles.

"The highest good is a mind that despises the operations of chance, rejoicing in virtue, or the power of the mind that is unconquerable, experienced in life, calm in action, and possessed of much kindness and concern for those whom it has dealings."

—Seneca

The above quote provides us with a few things we can contemplate. Let our strength of fortitude bring forth the mental toughness and resilience needed for us to ascend towards the attainment of wisdom. Let our minds be unconquerable.

Conduct of Reason

"The despicable phoniness of people who say, 'Listen, I am going to level with you here.' What does that mean? It should not even need to be said. It should be obvious—written in block letters on your forehead. It should be audible in your voice, visible in your eyes, like a lover who looks into your face and takes in the whole story at a glance. A straightforward, honest person should be like someone who stinks: when you are in the same room as him, you know it. But false straightforwardness is like a knife in the back. False friendship is the worst. Avoid it at all costs. If you are an honest and straightforward person and mean well, it should show in your eyes. It should be unmistakable."

—Marcus Aurelius

As the chapter heading suggests, we are going to be discussing three concepts within this chapter. Each of these could easily support its own chapter but are here combined for the purpose of improving one's thinking processes. Critical thinking can provide the grounding to sound reasoning, which here in part we shall use to lightly explore metaphysics as well. These three concepts applied together can greatly improve one's ability to see things as they really are. This supports the theme throughout this book of encouraging you to look at things from a different angle and widen the scope of your perception. The goal is to help you discover some situations and issues that many people face within the modern world that Stoic concepts can be applied to, rather than simply leaving you to work this out for yourself. After you've been presented with examples of how these concepts can be applied in modern times, you will become more familiar with these concepts to the extent that you will be able to apply them to any situation accordingly.

These concepts can be applied to situations at varied degrees in order to correctly address the adversity that you are personally facing. In this chapter, we will briefly touch on how to apply Stoic concepts in the face of adversity, with a general view of gaining insight from the Stoic way of thinking.

Firstly, we shall examine the above statement by Marcus Aurelius, which will help us attain a deeper understanding of some aspects of Stoic thinking. Being able to read people correctly is also part of the concept of looking at the world for what it is, allowing us to see things as they truly are and not be fooled into seeing them as something they are not, even if it's not as we wished things to be. Wisdom is needed to develop the skills to look within and find the strength to attain the ability to correctly see the world for what it is. Thus, reading people correctly and seeing the world for what it is can help us progress to new heights in our journey towards becoming a sage, which in Stoicism is one who is always able to see the truth.

In the modern world, phoniness is plentiful, thus becoming a sage is needed now more than ever. To do so, one must apply all the concepts discussed throughout this book and will certainly need the critical thinking skills to see the external world for what it is. As an example of modern phoniness, research studies and academics will often produce results that suit those who paid them to find those very results. The most notable example that comes to mind is that sports drinks were found to hydrate the body faster than water. Then, some years later, another study found the opposite to be true. There are many more examples of this, which are too many to list here. In addition, much of the media presents only a certain point of view on matters.

Stoicism divides all matters into two categories: those that are not under our control, thus we are not asked to judge, and those that are under our control. Critical thinking skills are certainly required to discern which things are placed into each category and to understand the underlying reasons for this decision. The Stoic concepts will assist as tools for such a task, thus leading to us gaining wisdom and improving our conduct towards the external world. We must remain mindful not to become like those who are phoney and not straightforward, as this is something that is quite infectious by its very nature. We have seen in our times that many have become like this. Here, then, is another opportunity to remove ourselves from the mob and join the ranks of the insane. As this idea emerges time and again in Stoicism, it can be called a concept of its own.

Stoic thinking emphasises the building of character, attaining higher levels of wisdom and judging the external world correctly. However, in the modern world, it is quite easy to fall into relying on groupthink and adopting ideas that are not necessarily our own but instead have been influenced by our peers and the media. Such ideas can be automatically internalised if one is not aware of such a thing happening. It is the task of the wise, then, to use their rationale correctly to gain a true understanding of anything that is presented to them.

When presented with an idea, one should be able to understand how such a conclusion was reached from its initial premise. In the modern world, we are often presented with simply the conclusion. It can also be helpful to see things from a broader context, perhaps drawing on different sources to formulate one's own opinions. The question arises as to whether, in the modern world, the majority lack the ability to correctly utilise their rationale, or if they have not been taught how to do so, using tools such as those the Stoics have imparted. Well, here we will look into the details of this issue.

We will move from discussing these matters in a broader sense to looking specifically at conflict resolution in our personal interactions with others, whether they are acquaintances, colleagues or more personal relationships. We can apply the context of higher ethics to our conduct towards others, once we have ascended to such positions with reason through Stoic philosophy. For instance, we may find ourselves in the midst of a conflict within an organisation that crosses relationship boundaries, which will require us to maintain an even mind if we are to navigate the situation correctly. The Stoics considered even-mindedness, which requires us to balance many factors from within ourselves and pressures from the external world, to be amongst the greatest of virtues. The Stoic is one who does not fear anything the external world presents. He is not afraid of pain, death, poverty or anything of the sort. The Stoic is only afraid of faltering on his moral responsibilities. With this outlook towards the external world, it becomes easier to deal with one's emotional stirrings or biases. We will discuss dealing with these things from different angles throughout the book, thus leading to a greater understanding of the human condition being attained.

As rational beings, we must strive for as much take as possible in order to see the truth. If the pursuit of truth is undertaken with biases, then it will only reveal half of the truth. This raises the question: at what degree of truth should one be satisfied? Too often, people are satisfied with finding only that which they seek, rather than the complete truth. It is very possible that the truth has evaded them, and yet they present to others what they found as if it were the whole truth. Although the average person might be satisfied by this, those who have ascended further along their path of seeing the world for what it is will acknowledge that they are only being presented with a partial truth and will continue to seek the complete truth alone. This is particularly important when pursuing the Stoic ideal of virtue, which is unlikely to be found in any such partial presentations.

For the most part, if we find ourselves involved in a conflict, it is a conflict either caused by our actions, by responding to another's actions, or a conflict between others that we are mediating. Regardless of how we find ourselves in a conflict, it is important to remain directed by virtue and keep an even mind throughout the process. By adopting a Stoic outlook and utilising the tools they have imparted, we can develop faster decision-making abilities, while remaining directed by virtue. Thus, in any kind of contention or conflict, however challenging, the Stoic is still able to live in accordance with nature rather than being influenced by a set agenda and or emotional state, as often happens to others during conflicts. As the path towards virtue is maintained, we can achieve positive outcomes most of the time, which is a worthy pursuit.

As one progresses through the philosophy and outlook of the Stoics, it will become something that radiates through their actions. Others can see and respect this, inspiring them to also ascend towards virtue. This makes it obvious to people that if they come to you for a resolution then one will certainly be found with wisdom and correct judgement, just as people approached the likes of Epictetus and Seneca for advice. All these points are connected, as again the fact that other people come to you for advice will make more people trust you, for they will think that surely you are one that seeks to see things as they are without being tainted with bias and incorrect perspectives. As noted in the earlier statement by Marcus Aurelius, your honest nature "should be unmistakable".

"When you have assumed these names—good, modest, rational, a man of equanimity, and magnanimous—take care that you do not change these names; and if you lose them, quickly return to them."
—Marcus Aurelius

There will be times when you are not correct in your understanding because someone outsmarts you, which is sometimes unavoidable—though with practice of all that is being discussed in this book, this becomes less likely. In other instances, your own biases may lead you to be unjust to some extent. If you realise this when reflecting on the situation, then try to correct your behaviour and make amends. This would be the virtuous and noble way, in which you remain malleable enough to always learn and see things as they really are. This shows humility and strength of character, something which will not go unnoticed by others and will earn you a level of respect. Remember that a diamond cannot be polished without friction to bring forth its beauty; similarly, a man cannot build his character without facing trials of adversity. Overcoming each obstacle will make your diamond shine brighter. Therefore, if you know that you have faltered in your interactions with others, it is prudent to quickly return to the right path. Be robust in your inner world and adaptable to the external world by maintaining an even mind, especially when it is difficult to do so. That is exactly when it will count most.

In any kind of personal conflict, whether in a business meeting or a disagreement between friends and family, one should seek to quieten the ego and remain even-minded. Overcoming adversity and understanding the situation correctly is key to obtaining valuable information and achieving your desired outcome in such a conflict. It can be advisable to let everyone involved take their time and speak as needed to get their message across. This will provide everyone involved with further insights into how things really are and allow you to judge the situation accordingly. Achieving mastery in this area will save much time in resolving such matters, which quite often present themselves in business and other situations. In business, such conflicts can come from sources either internal or external to the organisation. Either way, one must deal with these matters swiftly to then be able to focus on furthering one's journey along the Stoic path.

Drawing on the wisdom we have attained along the journey thus far as well as Stoic principles, we will be better equipped for conflict resolution. Our experiences and philosophical grounding will enhance our ability to deal with any form of conflict, wherever it comes from, while remaining directed by virtue. Understanding the complete situation is essential. Many people falter in this regard due to their biases and preconceptions, leading them to miss details that may have changed their perspectives. It is important to make such people aware of the information they were not aware of in order to help them ascend to a better position. However, sometimes, when people realise they do not know something, their pride makes them act in ways which hinder their progression to whatever you were enlightening them towards, meaning that even after being presented with further insight regarding the complete picture, they will still hold their initial opinion. In such cases, don't let this trouble you.

When facing internal conflict within an organisation, at times people may look upon you as a difficult person and push back against what you are offering. In response, you must fortify yourself like an impenetrable fortress by being moderate and taking a middle-ground approach with temperance. You should not be too kind or harsh with them. It is vital to resolve issues quickly and save time, as these situations often repeat. The techniques you choose to harness will be a determining factor in how swiftly you can resolve conflicts and resume progress along your journey.

A first-principles thought process should be used, in which each part of the discussed matter is broken down into its simplest of parts, and then you can build up from there. With this kind of method, there is no room for misrepresentation of anyone's version of events. It also prevents others from trying to outsmart, confuse or emotionally manipulate the situation, all of which will hinder the resolution or at least lengthen discussion, thus wasting much time.

Dealing with a conflict involving people in higher positions than you requires a different approach. While you should not think your desired results are out of your reach, remember that people in higher positions may have less patience with you. Therefore, it is essential to maintain discipline, as they may try to provoke an emotional response from you, which would inevitably put you at a disadvantage and move you quickly away from the favourable tide you had wished for. By keeping in mind the direction you want to go, with wisdom and discipline, you will ensure the tide turns in your favour at some point in the discussion.

It is important to recognise that people you respect may not respect you. In such a situation, you should learn to be your own hero. If instead you try to be like them, you will never achieve this. At most, you will only be a reflection of them, meaning that you have given them permission to say what you can and cannot become. This is not aligned with the Stoic principles, which advise you to look within to find strength. By seeking validation from others, you will not be able to look within without your self-reflection being tainted by their biases. The best place to get validation is from your own logic and philosophy, which, if used correctly, will present you with the answers you seek.

Be willing to take some risks in discussions with those in higher positions than you but remain calculated whilst doing so. Remain forthcoming with the respect they deserve.

It may simply be that they do not understand the position you are coming from or the details of the work you are tasked with. However, if you believe that your actions, based on your knowledge and experience, are moving the organisation forward in the right direction, then continue to pursue them. Communicating details to the higher-ups that they may not have been fully aware of may help to bring forth a resolution, as once the details are understood by everyone involved, the team should be once again aligned in the same direction.

One must always seek the knowledge and ask oneself, "How do I get better?", just as the student does. We should not think that we are masters, even when we have reached the levels at which mastery truly does operate. Be flexible and recognise that there's always another level of mastery to reach. Be disciplined to maintain progress on this path, applying the concepts of Stoicism along the way. Seek out counsel from mentors and people who are better than you or who have, in their own way, travelled further than you. At the same time, embody your philosophy in such ways that others can notice, and teach others where you can; this will enable you to learn twice. Be the best version of yourself you can be in order to overcome any adversity within your organisation. Adopting a Stoic mindset will help you to take meaning from and make sense correctly of the external aspects of this world. Foster a calm inner strength; it will serve you well towards virtue.

The Stoics used their thoughts and actions to serve others. Therefore, you should use compassion to reiterate all points of view within a meeting and ensure everyone has been heard to their satisfaction. This will help you to draw conclusions that have a lasting impact on the organisation's success and ensure that each individual clearly understands their role in taking the organisation forward and what is required of them.

An approach to take could be to stop thinking of yourself as being in competition with others. Be instead in competition with yourself, and look within to find the answer to how far you can go to seek out your true potential. As the saying goes: if you are going at all, then go all the way. Do not give up; do not give in. Be relentless in your pursuit.

Nothing of any real substance comes easy. We will inevitably face resistance, and resilience is often required to overcome the challenges we face along the way. But we will find gifts along this path as well, between the obstacles, and we should appreciate each one as it comes. After each one, we will find ourselves a bit further along the path we set out on.

Gone are the days of heroic leaders. We must take care to understand the people and environments we find ourselves with. If we do this, it may help us to align ourselves with where nature intended us to be, and more often, we will find ourselves doing the right thing.

From Knowing Nothing
to Much More and Back to Again
Knowing Nothing

When I first started my journey on the Stoic path, I did not know much. I studied on a daily basis to learn those concepts that are concerned with the aspects of the inner and external realms, for the purposes of building character from within and bringing about change for the better in the external world, and then moved on to the broader concepts. I always kept the question alive in my mind: *How can I get better?* The answer was to regularly monitor my progress. Even small steps along the path each day made all the difference. Noticeable progress started to present itself, and problems that once seemed insurmountable started to be solved. As I progressed further along the path, answers that were once elusive now presented themselves quite instantly. This progress was due to the embodiment of Stoic concepts, which helped ensure I took the correct actions towards the external world.

If you work on the concepts within this book, you too will see signs of attaining this same progress. On this path, you can become an executive, although in another realm, who can deal with anything the external world presents to them. To be called an executive, one must execute a certain number of tasks per day, and these concepts for the ordering of the mind are the very tools that will help you do this.

The only problem is that once you accept that you are a master of your craft, then you can adopt a rigid mindset in which the master thinks they know everything there is to know. The solidification of your identity as a master can lead to a lack of flexibility when the situation demands it. Therefore, the Stoics considered the journey towards mastery as the goal, rather than mastery itself. In today's fast-changing world, we need to be adaptable without compromising upon our principles. To remain as malleable as you once were at the start of your path, you should approach learning as a student even after mastery has been attained, striving to become a bigger and stronger version of yourself with wisdom. Being a student served you well along the path to mastery, and it would be wise to continue with this mindset no matter how far you have progressed. This will allow you to once again have that flexibility necessary to reach new heights. Many a wise man towards the end of his life has said that he now knows that he does not know much. Perhaps then we can take the wisdom from this as foresight to know that if we ever reach such places, we should not stop there.

The contrast between the world of the ancient philosophers and the modern times in which we find ourselves is stark, particularly with all the technological advancements we have made. Despite this, the Stoic view of the aspects of the inner self and the external world remains much the same. Along the Stoic path, we can continue to gain wisdom that helps us deal with challenges and uncertainties we may encounter. In our constantly changing environment, we must constantly adapt in order to survive and thrive. To do this, we must operate within this context with certainty and consistency, thinking correctly and making sound decisions at the fast pace demanded of us. We must focus on what really requires a response and what is just external noise that we are safe to ignore, for not all things require our judgement.

The Stoic mindset requires us to not be reactionary when dealing within, but to have a deeper understanding of the people and situations within it that may try to control how we react in ways that are more useful to them and not to us. The wisdom of the Stoics can help us to conduct ourselves accordingly in such situations.

Marcus Aurelius once said, "If there is no enemy from within, then no enemy from outside can harm us." This statement shows us that no matter the situation, if we are not our own biggest critic, then the criticism of others may not move us.

How will you stay strong and maintain a clear mind and vision to keep traversing forwards in the face of pitfalls and obstacles? Perhaps with the mindset shown in the following poem:

The Rudyard Kipling poem "If—", one of my favourites, is a great example of Victorian-era Stoicism. I shall present it here and attempt to add my own comments after each statement, while also including Stoic quotes to show you where Kipling's inspiration perhaps came from.

> *If you can keep your head when all about you*
> *Are losing theirs and blaming it on you;*

The Stoic thinkers believed it was better to remove yourself from the masses and join the ranks of the insane. Adding to this: look within to find strength. Be the immovable mountain when all fingers are pointing towards you. To be even-minded is the greatest of virtues.

"You have power over your mind. Not outside events. Realise this and you will find strength."

—Marcus Aurelius

If you can trust yourself when all men doubt you,
But make allowance for their doubting too;
If you can wait and not be tired by waiting,
Or being lied about, don't deal in lies,
Or being hated, don't give way to hating,
And yet don't look too good, nor talk too wise;

Know your philosophy and be metaphysically grounded within. Trust in yourself, but have the wisdom to allow for doubting too, in case there is some truth within what others have to say. Be in the present and do not worry about the past or future. Do not become like your enemy.

"Look well into thyself; there is a source of strength which always springs up if though wilt always look."

—Marcus Aurelius

If you can dream—and not make dreams your master;
If you can think—and not make thoughts your aim;
If you can meet with Triumph and Disaster
And treat those two impostors just the same:
If you can bear to hear the truth you've spoken
Twisted by knaves to make a trap for fools,
Or watch the things you gave your life to, broken,
And stoop and build 'em up with worn-out tools;

The Stoics recommended having sharp mental faculties and utilising creativity and imagination without getting carried away by them. You should be able to re-centre as needed to deal with reality. Compared to other, more academic philosophies, Stoicism is more practical, and its concepts can be applied in thought and then in action. Triumph and disaster are both external events, thus make no difference to the Stoic thinker. You should not be materialistic and should recognise that none of your material possessions will come with you to the grave, so therefore, you should rather focus on achieving excellence.

"Very little is needed to make a happy life, it is all within yourself in your way of thinking."

—Marcus Aurelius

If you can make one heap of all your winnings
And risk it on one turn of pitch-and-toss,
And lose, and start again at your beginnings
And never breathe a word about your loss;

This quote further emphasises that one should not value material possessions above all else. Although the specific action in this example is not advised, just that you should have the mindset to do so—"if" is the keyword. The example presents a difficult situation—how could you not even speak a word of it if this happened to you? Well, a Stoic could.

"Loss is nothing else but change, and change is nothing but nature's delight."

—Marcus Aurelius

If you can force your heart and nerve and sinew
To serve your turn long after they are gone,
And so hold on when there is nothing in you
Except the Will which says to them: 'Hold on!'

If such a thing did happen to you, you are still able to remain the immovable mountain. Even though you may not have said a word of it, others may still have been informed; you will remain resilient, and the message you have for the world is: "Hold on. I will be back."

"Perfection of character is this: to live each day as if it was your last, without frenzy, without apathy, without pretence."

—Marcus Aurelius

If you can talk with crowds and keep your virtue,
Or walk with Kings—nor lose the common touch,
If neither foes nor loving friends can hurt you,
If all men count with you, but none too much:

Those who speak with crowds are usually of some importance, and if you are such a person, you should not let this make you pompous. You should keep virtuous and humble even if you walk with kings, to remember where you came from. Also note that positions of power are just like material possessions, which may not last.

Foes or friends can only hurt you if you choose to let them. You should serve humanity in accordance with nature, and not be weighed down if others attempt to make you act in ways that are not in accordance with nature.

"First rule is to keep an untroubled spirit. The second is to look things in the face and know them for what they are."

—Marcus Aurelius

If you can fill the unforgiving minute
With sixty seconds' worth of distance run,
Yours is the Earth and everything that's in it,
And—which is more—you'll be a Man, my son!

The one who learns to master himself does not react even to the most significant of adversities and remembers that between action and reaction, there is space for decision. If you can find these spaces and use them to judge and act accordingly, then you are well on your way to becoming a Stoic.

Endurance

"True worth is eager for danger, and gives thought to its aim, not what it will endure, as even what it will endure is a part of its renown. Warriors glory in their wounds, and delight in displaying the blood that was spilled in better fortune: those who return unscathed from battle may do the same, but the wounded survivor attracts more eyes."

—Seneca

Endurance is a central tenet of Stoicism and is often mentioned throughout the literature. In the above quote, Seneca demonstrates how warriors were motivated by glory and were willing to endure the processes of war to achieve it. How may we take wisdom from such a statement and apply it to our own experiences so that we may find the will to endure all that it takes to progress? Well, we must realise that nothing shall be attained without adversity, and on any path, failure is one such danger. We must face our dangers with a similar eagerness as Seneca's warriors. You may not be on the battlefield, facing the same dangers, yet the dangers that lie ahead of you are dangers all the same. Once we recognise these dangers, we must give thought to our aim in facing them. This will create the mindset that we are willing to overcome those dangers that lay ahead, as our will is aligned with the eagerness to reach our desired aim and we have the tools and plan in place to traverse the road ahead.

This brings our attention to the idea of endurance, as plenty of this will be needed along this journey for those that wish to set upon the Stoic path. Those of us on this path must face additional challenges, both inwardly and outwardly, compared to those who are not pursuing such a path.

How, then, does one last the distance without burning out mentally? Well, this is why it is not recommended to rush the attempt to ascend to the mastery of such an endeavour. If you skip over many aspects of this philosophy without fully grasping them, it will be of less value to you. This path asks for deeper insight into oneself than many people are willing to do. They are not in pursuit of building their character in the ways in which the Stoic path requires.

My intention with this book is to present this very thing to a wider audience. One does not have to immerse themselves in the academic realms of this school of thought to achieve such things. Rather, Stoicism is readily available to those who are looking to better themselves and the external world around them in a more practical way. It provides those on the Stoic path with the tools they can use to deal with both their inner and external worlds, while remaining directed towards virtue.

Endurance is needed to achieve success in many pursuits, but it is particularly vital for those pursuing mastery of the Stoic path. This path presents many different challenges, in particular the many different facets of dealing with the inner and external worlds, that require endurance to overcome. It is important to be aware that life and time will continue regardless of your progress or lack of it on this path; the only way to advance upon the path is to put in the work along the journey.

The core concepts of Stoicism are very much interconnected, and there are a multitude of concepts we can draw upon to assist with building endurance. One such concept is the practice of self-inflicted hardship, as was practised by the Stoics, which can help prepare the mind in advance for when adversity presents itself by building fortitude and resilience, which will help to cultivate the endurance necessary to remain on course when faced with such adversity. Self-inflicted hardship serves as a method to gain foresight into potential challenges that lie ahead, while endurance is the actual method that will assist in overcoming any such adversity.

Another Stoic concept that can be utilised in the pursuit of endurance is *amor fati*, or the acceptance of one's fate. However, this acceptance does not encourage a passive mindset, for to realise your fate, you must first fully embody the qualities required by the Stoic path and commit your very best efforts towards your desired outcomes. Once all such attempts have been exhausted, then one can then rest, satisfied, with *amor fati*, as the Stoics did. A particular mindset is required for this. One must have the wisdom to discern what is within one's power to change and what is not, as this will determine when one can rest and accept their fate. It requires foresight, insight and wisdom to know one's capabilities and the challenges ahead.

At this point we could apply *amor fati* and accept our current situation, or we can push ourselves to take that one more step that could make all the difference to reach for that which we aimed to attain that is just outside our reach, and only then truly accept *amor fati* and be truly satisfied by taking such a position. Our will and endurance will assist in this process, particularly towards the end of it. Thus, we should be aware of this concept in the same way as self-inflicted hardship, as both can provide similar kinds of results only if utilised correctly. We can combine this with the concept of looking within, as that is where our will resides, even when taking that one more step towards overcoming adversity is a matter of the external world.

Incorporating the concept of *amor fati* into your pursuit of virtue on the Stoic path is thus itself demonstrating the mental toughness to know that you are only capable of changing things within your control and that you should find the opportunities to rest a short while and fully contemplate the lessons you have learned for the journey ahead. Endurance is required every step of the way, as the journey itself is the goal. It is the ever-ongoing task of the wise to embrace the journey to its fullest potential.

In today's world, distractions are plentiful, and a certain kind of endurance is needed to remain focused on our goals. In such a context, the concepts of discipline and endurance can be combined. In discussing the connectivity and inter-relatedness of these two concepts, a clearer picture should start to form in the mind of the reader of what these concepts can provide. To achieve mastery of the Stoic path, we should understand how to combine the use of various concepts to achieve a better result in the face of adversity. It is advisable to first understand each concept individually, and then move on to combining them. Utilising the Stoic concepts in combination with endurance will lead to even greater results available to those upon this path.

There are elements of life that everyone indulges in, even though they are not part of the Stoic path. I am referring here to wasting our time, socialising much more than necessary and finding many things to entertain us. In the modern world, we have social media where we can keep scrolling endlessly. We have video games that take to months to complete. All such modern forms of entertainment, along with literally just being social, do not contribute to building our character and are in opposition to Stoic wisdom. Ask yourself what percentage the Stoic teachers would dedicate to leisurely pastimes compared to that which they dedicate to their journey. The answer to this arrives swiftly to anyone who knows even just a little about the Stoics. For, certainly, the majority of their time would be dedicated towards the journey.

It should by now be clear that building our character directed towards virtue will require much endurance. Endurance is the concept that is working behind the scenes, assisting us in many regards along our Stoic journey. It is the very thing that we apply to take that one more step needed to reach our goals.

Endurance can also be required to achieve the Stoic principle of living in accordance with nature. To do this, we must first look inwards to ourselves, then to what is going on in our immediate surroundings, and then beyond this to nature as whole. We must look at these three realms individually, then see how they are connected as part of a whole. Each must be worked on in sequence, yet we must understand the connections between them. It should be clear that this journey is not short. Rather, it is a great journey, and only a few will ever approach its horizon. We should know this and maintain our motivations to follow this path. Each individual will have their own reasoning to continue with this sort of mindset.

As we progress towards this horizon, it will seem that the closer we get, the further it remains from us. Thus, the journey becomes the destination, and the obstacles we encounter along the way become part of the process.

Building our character is a task that the wise undertake with the knowledge that it does not really have an end. Similarly, few Stoic concepts have a fixed end goal. Their ending comes when we decide that we have attained our desired goals.

Undertaking this journey is a noble endeavour, and at times we may need to rest along the way while remaining steadfast. The Stoics advised us to be like a cliff face. The waves may come with varying softness or strength, but they must eventually return whilst the cliff remains firm. To remain so firm against the various things within the external world that attempt to shake or move us from our desired positions will surely require endurance. This applies whether we are in motion on our ascent or if we simply desire to remain still. The pursuit of wisdom does not come swiftly to anyone. Only after acquiring knowledge and putting it into practice can one truly advance towards wisdom.

There are many more concepts we can discuss to highlight the importance of endurance as a key element of Stoicism. With this knowledge, it would be prudent for us to keep it in mind along our own journeys.

"I once provided Aristophanes with subject matter for his jokes, the entire company of comic poets has showered its barbs of poisoned wit upon me: the very means they used to attack my virtue made it shine out more; for it suits it to be brought in the public eye and put to the test, and no men understand how great it is better than those who have come to know its strength by assailing it: the hardness of flint no men know better than those who strike it."

—Seneca

The above quote shows the response that wise men from the past were often met with when they presented their wisdom to the people. Throughout history, many have come and gone who spoke the truth, and yet they faced the very same adversity that is being noted by Seneca above. There could be many reasons for this, and it is important to consider the different contexts in which these individuals existed, but for the focus of our discussion, let us see that one thing they all had in common is that they were seeking the truth or possessed the truth. Subsequently, their wisdom often involved the limiting of pleasure in some regards. Upon hearing this, people tend not to take to it well and use all kinds of methods to resist these callings. One such method is to use ridicule. This kind of ridicule can either be directed towards the concepts they are being presented with or the person articulating the concepts to them. We can see in the above quote how Seneca endured such an onslaught of ridicule in front of an audience; outwardly presenting an emotional reaction to such ridicule may cause the faltering of one's character.

Mastering endurance can help us better face adversity. This is especially relevant in today's society. All around us, we can see that we have become very reactionary. Society lets us know that it is fine to let our emotions be free and there is no need to keep them domesticated in the way the Stoics have recommended. Though this can be healthy for the most part, it can leave those that have adopted such a method of thinking vulnerable when faced with adversity, leaving them in a position where they may not be able to overcome a particular obstacle. This kind of situation has the potential to cause lasting damage.

Further to this, once a person is affected emotionally then their perception and judgements cannot operate at their optimum levels. Allowing oneself to enter this kind of state can lead to faltering from any position currently held, thus causing possible regret in the long run. In the above quote, we can see all of this being avoided by Seneca with soundness of reason.

Seneca here demonstrates logic in the subtle sense, in that he had the wisdom to know that virtue was itself superior to whatever values the poets and comics actually held. Thus, he was pleased that this situation allowed the audience to witness how the value the Stoics hold as their highest good could not be effectively challenged to any degree. This enabled the audience to reach a rational decision as to who was correct in this scenario. So, within this example, we can see Seneca demonstrate logic, endurance, resilience and fortitude. He had already applied logic before this encounter to arrive at the belief that virtue is the highest good. He demonstrated endurance by keeping his emotions domesticated while being ridiculed in front of an audience, and in return was able to demonstrate the loftiness of virtue. Fortitude and resilience were demonstrated throughout this process to arrive at the desired outcome.

No matter what philosophical standpoint he was confronted with, Seneca would have been able to deal with it accordingly, as he had already carried out the works to build his character prior to entering such a debate. He would surely have put his own beliefs through many rigours to claim its superiority regarding the Stoic positions over what the other philosophical schools had to offer. So here we can see how if one has the endurance to build their character and beliefs, they can become like the cliff that stands firm against the waves. I did find some humour in imagining how poets and comics really must have experienced the toughness of flint after such an encounter with Seneca.

There are many stories, legends and historical accounts of the noble and courageous figures who faced similar challenges to those Seneca discussed. Though these figures often had truth on their side, the challenges they faced often seemed insurmountable. They often faced ridicule from the masses, as it is characteristic for them to reject new ideas that are presented to them. But when these characters faced stronger physical adversity that goes beyond mere words, and emerged victorious, the masses often reconsidered the correctness of their ideas. Perhaps this is why the Stoics said that it is better to remove ourselves from the masses and join the ranks of the insane. In the modern world, we no longer live in the age of the sword, but we can still take knowledge from ancient teachers such as the Stoics. Exchange of information and ideas is in a sense more prevalent than ever, in particular with the rise of the internet, and we will often find our own ideas met with similar negativity as the Stoics did.

We can apply the tools of the Stoics to help us overcome similar adversity for ourselves. That one more step that we have the endurance to take may very well be the last step needed to overcome an obstacle.

***

We can find satisfaction in dealing with that which is in our control while remaining calm when dealing accordingly with what is not in our control. This may not be an entirely uphill journey, especially with regard to the feeling we get when an obstacle has been overcome and we can see what progress we have made. There are those who actually look forward to being in this position time and again due to the satisfaction this feeling provides. We can feel this same satisfaction as we liberate ourselves and become more free, as the philosophers were, as we can remember how we were before and see just how much progress and improvement we have made. To reach such a point, endurance is required, especially during challenging moments.

A more advanced method is to seek other things within our inner and external worlds that we can make part of what we do control so that we may be even more effective in overcoming adversity. By utilising the concept of *amor fati*, we can acknowledge what things in our lives we do not have control over. For example, fortune is not something that can be relied upon. It is only what we do or think that can be relied upon. This kind of thinking can present us with a more satisfying life as we can always choose to better ourselves or our actions to move towards our goals and are then less likely to be disappointed.

Gratitude is a useful concept that can help us build endurance as it provides a positive outlook and the energy to continue the path. If we are sincere in our gratitude then it will be very valuable, as our gratitude for the things that we do possess, the progress we've made along our journey and the things we have had the opportunity to experience will provide us with strength and joy along the way. If we do the opposite and forget this very thing, we shall not have the necessary resolve and endurance to call upon, and it will always feel like an uphill journey. If we ever feel dissatisfied on our journey, then rather than trying to overcome this obstacle with even more endurance, we can first lighten its burden through gratefulness.

At first glance, on the surface, Stoicism can seem simple and appealing, but it requires endurance to pursue it on a deeper level, which may put some people off pursuing this path in the first instance. However, those who take on this pursuit will certainly experience more benefits than we can list here. It can be said that the true value of this philosophy is most apparent to those who are already familiar with it or who are in pursuit of a deeper understanding of its wisdom. It can also be considered a rite of passage as they had in ancient times, intended to build one's character. However, this process is self-imposed rather than led by others.

Endurance is crucial to getting through all of the concepts and principles of Stoicism and understanding them, and is then vital to actually being able to apply these things we have learnt in real time when faced with real adversity or situations that require us to present to the external world a higher level of our character. Once we have practised applying these concepts within our lives, we shall indeed find nuances within them and will inevitably personalise them to suit our own situations, which leads to a deeper understanding and level of wisdom.

"Do not disturb yourself by picturing your life as whole; do not assemble in your mind the many and varied troubles which have come to you in the past and will come to you in the future, but ask yourself with every present difficulty: What is there in this that is unbearable and beyond endurance?"

—Marcus Aurelius

Being in the present moment and focusing on the task at hand will, to some extent, make mustering endurance less arduous. At times, it can be challenging to think about enduring the whole journey, so it's helpful to think in smaller increments. Gather only the smaller amount of endurance needed for the particular obstacle you are facing rather than the whole endeavour. This will prevent you from overexerting yourself, while not losing sight of the bigger picture—a task related not to endurance but rather wisdom.

The Stoics emphasise the importance of the present, as the present is all that we really have. We can use their teachings to help us let go of worries about the past and future, freeing us to act more effectively within the present. By compartmentalising the challenges we face, we can focus on taking appropriate action in the moment.

We will find that something that initially seemed insurmountable now presents new possibilities for us to overcome it. These answers will be found specifically by those of us who are upon the Stoic path and have carried out the work required for understanding, practise, and acquisition of Stoic wisdom. We can combine all these things together and go even further than we could before. By cultivating resilience, fortitude, mental toughness and endurance, we can make a significant difference, as has often been mentioned by the Stoic teachers.

Stoicism and Critical Thinking

Critical thinking is quite often associated with the teachings of Socrates. Though not quite a Stoic himself, Socrates was nonetheless a renowned philosopher in his own right. Although Stoic literature does not explicitly highlight critical thinking as a stand-alone set of skills, it is evident that the Stoics utilised and implemented these skills to a high standard. Many of the Stoic concepts, for example, overcoming adversity, will greatly require this skillset. If one is to swiftly overcome obstacles, whether internal or external, then critical thinking will be vital. These issues may otherwise remove our peace of mind, which is troubling in its own right and can also slow progress on our journey and prevent us from working on other concepts at our fullest efficiency, leaving us with less-than-desired results in all these other aspects as well. This highlights the importance of resolving these issues as soon as possible with the tools at our disposal, including critical thinking.

Another perspective on this concept is to view problem-solving skills as existing in levels, each suited to solving different types of problems. It would be prudent to ask yourself whether you have enough problem-solving skills to deal with a wide spectrum of problems. Whether the answer is yes or no, you should realise the need to increase such abilities by utilising the tools offered by the philosophers. Whilst increasing the levels of your problem-solving skills, you will attain wisdom of many of the Stoic concepts discussed throughout this book and will have the insight and wisdom to know which combination of concepts to use depending on what is in front of you.

Critical thinking is an important skill to possess as it will enhance your understanding and help you find answers to both simple and complex questions, whether they're about daily life or deeper philosophical matters. This process will help you to gather facts, evidence, observations and any other relevant factors to arrive at the correct answers, then enabling you to make sound judgements about them. This allows you to arrive at informed conclusions without being influenced by personal biases and prevents you from acting like the Sceptics and constantly rethinking your conclusions, due to the rigours of this process.

Self-discipline is an essential aspect of Stoic teachings. Once you start using the Stoic concepts, including those within this chapter, it is up to you to continue until you have either arrived at wisdom with soundness or start to find yourself at the doors of the Sceptics. Whilst these are concepts that have been tested with the rigours of time, few people are aware of how to utilise them correctly. By widening the possible audience of such ideas, the external world will ultimately become a better place. I have personally carried out the works of the inner self, and this book is my second step in the process of looking within and finding strength, and then looking at the external world to see it for what it really is and work towards its betterment. Attempting such a thing without self-discipline will result in an inability to ascend to the truth with complete coherence; you will inevitably only discover part of the whole. It may be that you are left missing parts of an answer, or taking a sceptical position, leading to constant reevaluation.

Self-discipline is of great importance in Stoicism, as it allows you to become independent by truly understanding these concepts for yourself. It is like teaching a man to fish rather than giving him a fish. Thought leadership is also required to transfer these concepts to the modern world. Although critical thinking can be practised independently, it can also be utilised when working as part of a team. In such a scenario, it is necessary to ensure that all team members understand the underlying principles of the methods being applied, to reach correct answers with the least amount of mistakes during the process.

We cannot be certain how prevalent mental health issues such as depression and anxiety were in the ancient world, but it is clear that they are very much widespread today. When we find ourselves faced with such issues, we should first identify whether they are caused by something from the realms of the inner self or the external world. This can be called the recognition of our impressions and what caused these impressions. Through such identification, we can focus on working on the appropriate area. By utilising Stoic concepts to overcome adversity, we can carry out this task accordingly.

Philosophy and critical thinking to overcome adversity are valuable tools for solving such mental health issues, whichever realm they arise from. If we look at what we actually have control of in this life, we shall realise that it is truly only our mind. To control such a thing to the best of our ability is a worthy pursuit, not just in academia and our professions, as dangers of all kinds can present themselves at any time, from anywhere. I am not referring to dangers like a tiger leaping out of the bushes, but rather the kind posed by manipulative people or that can come with adopting opinions that do not adhere to one's principles of philosophy or of simply following popular opinion without checking whether it is built on stable and rational premises.

In today's society, people often look up to celebrities and try to emulate them rather than building their own character from the ground up. The problem with this approach is that they only see the end result and are missing much of the information and work required to get to that point. For example, athletes often mention that actually competing in an event is the easy part. Rather, the hard part is the 4 a.m. runs and daily practice. Therefore, if we try to emulate a celebrity without a strong foundation for this approach, we may not be able to withstand adversity when it presents itself. Any success achieved in such a way is built on unstable ground. To prevent such a situation, it is important to focus on building our character.

Whether we intentionally work on our character or we find ourselves facing much adversity by chance, it is important to do so rather than ignore this aspect. By doing so, we may discover things we did not intend to see, or weaknesses we were not aware of. It is important to remember that no one is perfect, and having the courage to discover such things can lead to greater wisdom. This is why we should set upon such paths, as they make us see things not as we wish to see them but rather as they are. Only when we see things as they really are can we do something about them correctly. This will take fortitude and resilience, as it will be a continual journey. However, when you look back and see all the many adversities you have overcome, that will be its own reward. But this journey does not finish there, as that is what will provide the fuel to keep going and ascend to new heights.

We spend a lot of time learning and developing skills for our careers and other endeavours, but how much time and work do we put in to working on ourselves? It is likely the answer is not enough. It is important to acknowledge that all the many other aspects of life, things like family, your career, your business and your finances will continue to demand time and energy every day. This means there will never be a perfect time to begin the journey of building your character. Therefore, there is no time better than the present to begin, and the concepts discussed within this book will certainly help you begin this journey.

"We need to bestir ourselves; life will leave us behind unless we make haste; the days are fleeing by, carried away at a gallop, carrying us with them; here we are making comprehensive plans for the future and generally behaving as if we had all the leisure in the world when there are precipices all around us."

—Seneca

Any adversity from any realm can be resolved by applying rigorous problem-solving techniques. Philosophy and critical thinking will speed up the process and play a significant part in arriving at answers more efficiently. The Stoic literature refers to this process not as problem solving, but rather all issues come under the umbrella of overcoming adversity. Further reading on critical thinking can be found outside of Stoicism for those that wish to explore the topic further. Progress through the Stoic teachings will most definitely develop one's critical thinking abilities as well as bring wisdom.

Perhaps some concepts are not fully explored within the Stoic literature due to the fact that ancient Stoic philosophers did not leave us with textbooks or similarly structured works. For example, Marcus Aurelius' *Meditations* were primarily notes written for his own reflection. Or Seneca's *Letters from a Stoic* is just that: a compilation of letters he wrote to people he knew. Epictetus' *Discourses* and the *Enchiridion* were compiled by a student of his who wrote down some of his lectures, originally for his own use.

If you study philosophy at university, you will be presented with a broader range of works to reference. No doubt you will encounter the works of Socrates and Plato, for example. Socratic questioning is the earliest form of critical thinking and lays the foundation for all later works on the topic.

I myself have taken the path of self-study and have drawn my own understanding and conclusions, which, although personal to me, can in many ways help other people build a sound foundation for their logic and rationale, build their character and encourage awareness and cultivation of Stoic principles. Unfortunately, the masses are not as aware of the benefits that can be gained from studying Stoicism as they could be. We can still take much wisdom from the Stoic literature, especially as we can clearly see the mindset these wise men displayed through their writings, which can become a powerful psychology to explore in our own lives. This is a valuable skill to possess for the journey of life, especially for those who have set upon the path of personal growth and character building. Stoicism is a subject of much significance, as the Stoic concepts really can be used within all fields of study.

Critical thinking is the intellectual discipline that allows one to move from an initial premise to a potential conclusion with soundness, having examined root causes, underlying reasons and the following premises along the way. It can be used to examine any subject more closely or to solve problems by breaking them down to their raw components in order to gain greater understanding. This could be used to evaluate two arguments to see which has the better-placed reasoning and sounder logic or to solve problems of any sort in some professions. For example, critical thinking can be used in the engineering profession to solve problems that arise during the design process, which may have come to a halt due to an unforeseen issue. Time and money are often being spent whilst such a problem persists, so engineers must use critical thinking to swiftly and effectively deal with the problem and move forward with the project. In such a scenario, the observations, evaluating of information, reflection, reasoning and analysis all have to be purposeful and self-regulating to reach the correct judgements.

"It is philosophy that has the duty of protecting us… without it no one can lead a life free of fear or worry."

—Seneca

Seneca's statement should be looked into properly to understand its deeper meanings. Philosophy is not a physical item such as a sword or shield that could protect us, so what does Seneca mean by this? The answer is quite profound. The ways that philosophy can protect us are part of what we will be discussing when we talk about building our character from the ground up using Stoic principles, which will enable us to overcome any adversity we may face from either the inner or external world. The second half of Seneca's statement regarding fear and worry provides insight into the first half. However, it is important to remember that this quote, like other sayings of the Stoics, is taken from a larger text. For me personally, when I look upon such a statement, I focus on the first part, which tells us what philosophy can do. I'll also take note of the second part, and if I am not currently experiencing fear and worry, I may think to myself: Can this idea be applied to what I am currently going through instead? For the most part, it probably can. Through looking at a quote in such a way, it comes to light that philosophy, and especially the concepts the Stoics have imparted to us, can assist us in dealing with so much more than it may seem at first.

Another way to look at this statement is that we are unique on this planet because we are rational creatures. It is only our rationality that makes us different from animals, and therefore, it is actually our duty to protect this amazing gift we have been given. Philosophy is just the tool to protect ourselves against irrationality. It allows us to truly look within ourselves and deal with the many challenges we face, allowing us to live a better quality of life. As the Stoics noted, it is the quality of our thoughts that determines the quality of our lives. Additionally, practising even-mindedness and moderation can help to eliminate our vices, thus enabling us to be better positioned to ascend to our fullest potential towards virtue.

The regular use of critical thinking should lead in some part to a shedding of certain aspects of us that were not serving us well in the first instance. As we become more familiar with these concepts, we can look within ourselves, which may happen quite instantly whilst reading Stoic literature or this book, as the content is thought-provoking, to say the least. However, to look within at a deeper level, it is best to do so intentionally. The concept of seeing things as they really are can also be applied here.

It can be overwhelming or scary to confront deeper-level issues within ourselves, but it is important to do so, even if we find things within ourselves that we are not fully ready or prepared to see. Applying Stoic concepts to the realms of our inner world will only lead us to the truth, and as noted by Marcus Aurelius, the truth never harmed anyone. Even if we were not ready to see a certain aspect of ourselves for whatever reason, it is better to deal with it by looking at it as an obstacle that has to be overcome to create a better path forward. The benefits of doing so will far outweigh leaving such a thing untouched. By being even-minded about it, we can remove the association between it and fear and anxiety, and ask ourselves why we sought to not see such a thing that was within us. Through such a task we will certainly attain new heights of wisdom, as we will know more about ourselves than we did before and will have dealt with an issue that may have been hindering us.

The modern world provides so many conveniences and comforts that it can seem like our purpose here is the pursuit of leisure, as was believed by the Epicureans. Well, this is certainly not the mindset of the one seeking to build their character, mental toughness and emotional resilience. These are two opposite mindsets that lead to different paths. The former tries to relax and enjoy life as much as possible, while the latter tries to strengthen themselves by facing as much adversity as possible and having the grit to get to where they want to, no matter what obstacles are present in front of them.

Those who seek to possess this powerful psychology and ascend to the heights of the full potential of their rationality shall indeed have many advantages over those who do not seek such things. Once you have reached the higher ground, where the views are breath-taking, satisfaction can be found by seeing how far you have progressed.

This may all just seem like common sense to you. If so, the question then arises: why are the masses not capable of this? If this is so "common", then why do the majority of people leave such an important thing behind to pursue other matters during their lives? Well, here we might find yet more wisdom, and understand why the Stoics advised us to remove ourselves from the masses.

"I view with pleasure and approval the way you keep on at your studies and sacrifice everything to your single-minded efforts to make yourself every day a better man. I do not merely urge you to persevere in this; I implore you to. Let me give you, one piece of advice: refrain from following the example of those whose craving for attention, not their own improvement, by doing certain things which are calculated to give rise to comment on your appearance or way of living generally."

—Seneca

In the modern world, there is so much focus on materialism, and while there is nothing inherently wrong with pursuing material possessions, it is equally important to focus on other aspects of your life, especially the realms of the inner self. For those who may at times be confused about such a comparison, after reading this book, put these thoughts through the rigours of the Stoic concepts as presented here. The Stoics believed in living in accordance with nature and virtue. Can one achieve this by acquiring all the items they desire, if such things help us to fit in and win the admiration of others? A way to look at this is to consider that if we remove certain elements from a framework, then is the framework still complete? If we focus only on the external world and neglect our inner world, then half of this philosophy has been left behind.

There are deeper meanings to things that we may miss if we focus only on the material aspects of the external world. While scientific methods are great instruments for discerning the workings of the external world, and most certainly the Stoics included physics within their epistemology, we should not rely solely on these methods to understand the world. To attain greater wisdom, we must use tools such as philosophy and logic with soundness of reason. Combining all such things correctly is a wise man's task.

The reflection we see of ourselves may not always represent the external world as it is, but rather as we wish it to be. The Stoics believed that seeking the clarity to see the world correctly required identifying and understanding the places where many of these concepts tie together, which enables people to conduct themselves within the external world correctly. By utilising the Stoic concepts and applying critical thinking, we can all arrive at our desired destinations on this path.

When using critical thinking, we should be mindful of our emotions, as these can affect how we think. It is important to remember our emotions are always at play. Keeping this in mind can give us the edge we need to endure parts of this journey that at times can get difficult. The Stoics teach us not to eliminate our emotions but rather to domesticate them. This requires knowing ourselves correctly and recognising how our emotions manifest themselves. There are many kinds of emotion that exist at varying levels, and exploring this would be an entire topic of its own.

In this regard, it is worth mentioning again that all the concepts discussed within this book are for the betterment of one's character. As an example of this, consider the fight or flight response that can trigger in our minds. If this response is triggered but not acted on, then perhaps fear or a similar emotion has stopped the person from being able to act accordingly and led to them faltering on this call to action. From this, we can attain the wisdom that any emotional message our mind presents to us should be taken as an indicator that we can choose to react to, rather than an emotional condition to remain under, which can hinder our ability to act swiftly when needed. This can be the very moment where emotional resilience is found. Such a task requires us to put our emotional reactions through the rigours of critical thinking in order to understand the underlying reasons how and why we do what we do. It is a process of self-discovery for the purpose of building one's character with strength and honour to overcome any adversity. This is the framework suggested by the Stoic school of thought in regard to such an undertaking.

Through such character building, you begin to internalise the Stoic principles needed to have mental toughness and emotional resilience in any situation. As noted by the Stoics, we often suffer more in our imagination than when we encounter the thing we feared in reality. Therefore, it is important to focus on keeping as many things as possible within our control in order to conduct ourselves within the external world.

It can be a challenging task to consistently identify which of our emotions are not serving us well. Along with emotions, our biases can lead to us failing to correctly understand or act within the external world. Because of this, the Stoics sought to domesticate their emotions to the best of their abilities and to remove their biases in order to see reality as it really is. Thus, it is the task of the wise to use all the tools in one's possession to deal with these matters of the inner self correctly.

"A single example of extravagance or greed does a lot of harm – an intimate who leads a pampered life gradually makes one soft and flabby; a wealthy neighbour provokes cravings in one; a companion with malicious nature tends to rub off some of his rust even on someone of an innocent and open-hearted nature – what then do you imagine the effect on a person's character is when the assault comes from the world at large? You must inevitably either hate or imitate the world. But the right thing is to shun both courses: you should neither become like the bad because they are many, nor be an enemy of the many because they are unlike you. Retire into yourself as much as you can. Associate with people who are likely to improve you. Welcome those whom you are capable of improving."

—Seneca

Although this is just a short excerpt from a longer letter, it highlights how following such a path can result in the acquisition of vices and the loss of virtues, even if we did not set out to do so. Negative traits can rub off on us through our active thoughts, or more commonly through emotional appeal. We do not fully formulate our thoughts about such things, which leads to our emotions getting the better of us and these things becoming a part of us. Therefore, it is recommended that we associate with those who can improve us or who we can improve, with the application of the Stoic principles.

We have demonstrated that this kind of rational thinking can be used for a vast array of things that can help with self-improvement. In particular, I like the way in which the application of Stoicism can be used for self-therapy. It provides so many useful teachings that, in most cases, practitioners of this philosophy really can be enabled to overcome just about any adversity.

We can use critical thinking to examine other philosophies and see they are rather different from Stoicism, in everything from their premises to conclusions. This allows us to decide for ourselves whether we believe Stoicism is the best philosophy for us to follow. Deciding to follow the Stoic path is something commendable. I hope that much of the reasoning throughout this book and my own personal journey have and will continue to be of much benefit to you.

The Importance of Logic and Reason

"Run always the short road, and Nature's road is short. Therefore say and do everything in the soundest way."

—Marcus Aurelius

As the saying goes, the shortest way from one place to another is in a straight line. The philosophers too agree with this, as we can see from this statement from Marcus Aurelius, although he is speaking in a broader context and combining this idea with the central Stoic principle of living in accordance with nature. The aim of the Stoic is to ascend from premise to conclusion as swiftly as possible without wasting time with sophistry, randomness and multiple premises. The Stoics were master logicians with a particular talent for the classification of things. This will be further detailed in this chapter and a subsequent chapter regarding Stoic metaphysics.

The concepts discussed in this chapter will benefit non-philosophy readers in their daily lives. Through application of these concepts to any kind of question or task, any person can become a practitioner of Stoicism and set themselves upon the path towards mastery. The concepts of logic and reason, closely linked with critical thinking and first principles, can help to improve our problem-solving skills in any context. As you progress along this path, you will greatly increase your ability to see things correctly, both within yourself and in the external world. With a solid grounding and familiarity in these concepts, you will have the keys to begin your Stoic ascent.

Incoherency and circular reasoning can lead to distraction from the higher kind of Stoic principles, and the tools and concepts introduced in this chapter can be used to avoid such things. Further to this, when others present us with emotional arguments, we can use logic to discern where such an argument might lead and thus swiftly and soundly deal with it, even though it did not come from a place of the same soundness. As we become more skilled in using these tools, we can begin to quickly identify and resolve such conflicts, to the benefit of all those involved.

Stoic literature provides many examples of how these tools can be used in various aspects of discourse, such as ethics, morality and dealing with adversity. By studying the Stoics, we can learn to apply their methodology to any task that similarly requires our attention.

Learning and implementing these concepts will improve our critical thinking, which requires sound logic and reasoning to come to rational conclusions. Such skills will enable us to face adversity and handle problems swiftly, thus increasing our ability to take on roles of greater responsibility, as such roles face a great variety and amount of problems and issues. The capabilities of Stoics in such positions can be seen in the examples of Marcus Aurelius as emperor and Seneca in the Roman Senate. This I mention to highlight how the Stoics sought to play high-ranking positions in society. It's worth noting this to dispel certain misconceptions regarding the Stoics in general.

The Stoic approach involves reflecting on the five principles of self-discipline, justice, courage, wisdom and virtue, among others. Once understood, all of these concepts are relatively straightforward to implement for those upon the Stoic path. Interestingly, in Stoic literature there are no complete books that wholly deal with just one or two of these concepts, as one might find in modern textbooks. Instead, most Stoic literature takes the form of short and concise writings within collections. This may be due to how it often takes the form of letters and discourses, or perhaps it is an indication of the Stoic style in getting to the point swiftly, as shown in the quote: "Run always the short road, and Nature's road is short."

If we too apply sound rationale to everything we do, as did the Stoics, it shall prompt us to instinctually and habitually work on that which can be improved in our lives. Thus adding to our perspective and giving us insight into the use of some of the tools we have acquired regarding logic, reason and soundness.

"Since it is reason which makes all other things articulate and complete, and reason itself must be analysed and made articulate, what is it that shall effect this? Plainly, reason itself or something else. That something else either is reason or it will be something superior to reason, which is impossible. If it is reason, who again will analyse that reason? For if it analyses itself, so can the reason with which we started. If we are going to call in something else, the process will be endless."

—Epictetus

The intent of the ancient Stoics was to swiftly move from a premise to a conclusion via sound reasoning and logic, rather than keep reevaluating like a Sceptic or presenting counter-premises. This, in my opinion, sets Stoicism apart from the other schools of thought, for it makes it appealing to the common man as well as to scholars.

In the modern world, many people believe that nothing is certain and anything is possible. For instance, if they were presented with the premise that a cup of tea could be made all by itself if nature was attempting such an activity, they would affirm that if nature was attempting such an activity, if attempted billions of times, there would be a possibility of it happening. However, this flawed reasoning fails to consider the multitude of complex steps involved in making tea, that would be impossible for nature to achieve alone, such as farming the tea, making the tea bags, bringing it to the kitchen, turning on the kettle, pouring the water into the cup, opening the fridge, taking out the milk and adding the milk—and not forgetting the sugar! Such flawed logic can be traced back to other philosophies which do not use sound reasoning to reach their conclusions but may be popular so people follow them without thinking it through for themselves. These philosophies may also present to them the idea that they should re-analyse the reason by which they came to any conclusion. As Epictetus noted, such a process of reevaluating will be endless. To avoid such flawed reasoning, it's important to study metaphysics, ontology and logic, for people who proclaim such things in the modern world would find their use of logic tested in this process. It could be said that they are lucky the Stoic teachers are no longer around to test them in such ways.

"When one of his audience said, 'Convince me that logic is useful,'
he said,
'Would you have me demonstrate it?'
'Yes.'
'Well then, must I not use a demonstrative argument?'
And, when the other agreed, he said, 'How then shall you know if I impose upon you?' And when the man had no answer, he said, 'You see how you yourself admit that logic is necessary, if without it you are not even able to learn this much—whether it is necessary or not.'"
—Epictetus

We can see from this quote that the use of logic and reason is useful for everyone whether they are aware of it or not. Logic and reason will inevitably provide much benefit to our lives, whether in a professional or personal context. It will assist in helping us find ideas to explore that are not illogical and irrational, which in turn will lead us to sounder conclusions.

Adopting this approach will most certainly benefit us by improving our problem-solving skills, our discourse in professional meetings, and our personal relationships, along with leading to a broader and deeper understanding of the universe we find ourselves in. Instead of viewing philosophy as merely an academic pastime, we should approach it with the intent of using it to work on ourselves mentally and emotionally and to reshape our principles and outlook on things. This approach was intended by the Stoic teachers, who recommend adopting it.

All the schools of philosophy use hypotheses to arrive at conclusions and employ tools such as logic and reason to develop their own brand of philosophy. Stoicism is just one of these schools of thought that makes use of logic and reason. This chapter is included for those who are new to philosophy or Stoicism, who will greatly benefit from becoming familiar with the concept of logic and seeing how the Stoics approached this concept within their thoughts and works. The Stoic use of logic was one of the two great systems of logic prevalent throughout the 3rd century. However, over time, Aristotle's version of logic became much more prevalent and remains so to this day.

The Stoic method of logic helps a person to see the actuality of the particulars contained within any given premise or conclusion in a discussion. This understanding allows them to use reason to navigate uncertainty and adversity in their practical affairs, standing their ground with logic and providing sound answers to either agree or disagree with what is being presented.

The Stoics considered logic to be the understanding of a wide range of things which are all interlinked, including epistemology, language, grammar, and the ways in which the universe works. Like all schools of philosophy, Stoicism follows certain rules of logic, such as the rule of non-contradiction, which states that something cannot simultaneously be right and wrong, or true and untrue, or possible and impossible.

The Stoics included speech within their understanding and use of logic, which can be further broken down into three aspects. The first is the sounds, or the spoken words themselves; the second is the actual words which are spoken within a language, though these are not regarded as the actual complete things that are being said. The third is the question or command that the words are used to construct.

I have kept the above description as straightforward as possible, as this particular topic can get quite scholarly. For if we delve too deep into this, it may not be an enjoyable read for those who are new to philosophy and Stoicism, though those who wish to read further into this can look into the Stoic literature itself. There are four kinds of modal properties, or ways of distinguishing an assertible statement: possible, impossible, necessary, non-necessary. When a Stoic analyses an argument, they use a form of deductive reasoning known as syllogism when what is being said contains more than two premises. The majority of the time, the initial premise will be something simple with a solid foundation, but the second and further premises do not have to be equally simple.

An argument typically falls into one of five categories: demonstrable, conditional, disjunction, negation conjunction and connectives. Stoic literature only touches upon defining these categories and swiftly moves on to discussing paradoxes. A paradox is a statement that contradicts itself. In ancient times, students of Stoicism, such as those studying under Epictetus, were intentionally given paradoxes to work with in order to test their reasoning capabilities. Students of philosophy must learn to soundly deal with paradoxes, and there have been many books written that examine specific paradoxes in detail. It is prudent to swiftly identify when such a thing is being presented to us and deal with it accordingly. This will prevent us from wasting our time on a complex paradox, as there is much work to be done on other things along the Stoic path instead. However, it is still advisable to become aware of Stoic logic and to be able to utilise critical thinking from first principles whenever situations require it of us.

The Stoics thought of logic as a gateway to self-insight, as human passions can often lead to error and misuse. Such passions can creep into our inner dialogue and make it logically incorrect. Logical reasoning can resolve this kind of issue. This method of inner work was used by the Stoics to maintain the soundness they desired.

"Most men are unaware that the handling of arguments which involve equivocal and hypothetical premises, and, further, of those which derive syllogisms by the process of interrogation, and, in general, the handling of all such arguments, has a bearing upon the duties of life. For our aim in every matter of inquiry is to learn how the good and excellent man may find the appropriate course through it and the appropriate way of conducting himself in it."

—Epictetus

In this quote from Epictetus, we can see several of the aspects we are discussing within this chapter. This quote can be seen as a summary of what is being discussed and is powerful in its brevity. It shows how the Stoics utilised hypothetical scenarios to discern the nature of a good man and how he should act in various situations. Surely, the Stoics believed that they were good men themselves, if they were to advise us on how to be this very thing.

A central theme within Stoicism is service to others. This too is demonstrated by the above statement from Epictetus, as serving others is one of the duties of a good man, though it is the exercise of one's will that steers a person towards holding Stoic principles. The statement from Epictetus demonstrates a way of reconciling the will not to be enslaved by others and the duty to serve them. Self-discipline carries us correctly towards our intentions, while simultaneously enabling us to resist being enslaved by things that present themselves from an emotional standpoint.

Epictetus frequently employed this style of questioning in his works, and many of Seneca's works share a similar style. Epictetus' works are called the *Discourses*, as they are records of actual discourses, and the nature of these texts might explain why the complete works have not survived to the present day. Back to the question itself, then—we may wonder if the question is being asked in order to reveal a flaw in the respondent's logic, depending on the answer received. However, given the style of the question, it does seem that the answer was known already before the question was even asked.

In today's world, with all the information we are constantly presented with from various media and social media platforms, the use of deductive logic can be incredibly useful. Through it, we can discern which information cannot stand the rigours of Stoic logic, simplifying the task of navigating an overwhelming amount of information.

Acquiring knowledge along the Stoic path will lead to an increase in wisdom. Even small improvements in logical reasoning can have a significant impact on our lives, like a ripple effect. Another benefit from improving our logical reasoning is that we will save time and energy in the decision-making process, as we will be able to arrive at conclusions with greater speed. As with any pursuit, expertise comes with experience.

Once such a skill has been gained for oneself, it can also be used to help others, such as friends, family or colleagues.

Another person may present some issue they are finding challenging, and you will immediately be able to start breaking down whatever their issue is and advising them on the right thing to do, much like is done in the letters and discourses of Seneca and Epictetus.

After any meeting, problem or situation encountered, you should record your progress to avoid forgetting important details later. At times of stress, confusion and chaos, you may not have time in the moment, but later you can review your journal and reflect on how the situation could have been better dealt with. None of those challenging things should make you feel weak, as you are equipped with the wisdom to deal with them and become a master. Even as a master, it is helpful to approach such situations with the outlook of the student, as the student is always looking to learn whereas the master thinks he knows everything.

By using a journal to make notes and retrospectively contemplate the situations you've faced, you'll be better equipped going forward. This allows you to better face difficult situations, even in times of pressure and in the fast-paced environment of the modern world. Mastering this through daily practice will inevitably help you lead yourself, your team and your family in the way that you desire.

In the modern world, mental health issues are prevalent, and many people experience common mental health issues that do not require medical attention. Perhaps people suffering from such issues just do not know how to think correctly. From talking to people with such issues, I have found that they are often struggling with unresolved matters that are thus leaving them in a constant flux of suffering. It is possible that understanding Stoic philosophy and applying Stoic logic to their situation would improve their conditions.

I do whatever I can to assist people who present such problems to me, which I can see does make a difference in their lives. However, the best solution would be for them to start thinking correctly by ordering the thoughts within their minds. One way to do this is to become familiar with thinking with logic and reason. This is one of the reasons I wrote this book, as Stoicism has helped me to face such adversity, and I believe it may help others do the same.

I am no expert on the subject of mental health, but I have seen improvements after introducing some people who suffer from mental health issues to Stoic thinking. They have also confirmed this. While Stoicism as a whole can help improve such issues, I believe that it is particularly worth taking from this school of thought the aspects dealing with the self and our conduct with others, especially if you do not intend to adopt the complete philosophy. However, if you have already gone deeper into Stoic philosophy and are familiar with Stoic logic, then it may be prudent to apply a more holistic approach to Stoicism. Unlike other forms of therapy, this involves us looking into the deeper meanings of this philosophy rather than dealing with the particular issue alone.

We all use some parts of logic in our daily lives without thinking much about it, but it can be a wise thing to study it just a bit further to then improve our skill with it. We are constantly exposed to different points of view, podcasts and debates in the media, but this is all subjective. By studying logic and reason, even just a little, we can make those small improvements in our logical analysis that place us in a better position than the masses. If we are dealing with complex and persistent challenges, then we can delve deeper into this subject to put ourselves on the trajectory towards overcoming them.

It is my opinion that the short introduction on logic and reason contained within this chapter can certainly assist anyone looking to further this skill to overcome adversity. The concepts can also be helpful if you're working on something and have reached a plateau but desire to make improvements to take things to a new level.

Some people are for the most part driven by their emotions. For such people, it can be a long road to start shifting their minds towards rationality and finding the right balance between their emotions and their mind, both of which are part of us and make us rational creatures. Societal conditioning and the use of emotional triggers in the media can push us towards being mostly emotional rather than logical, which is especially a risk for those who have not studied logic and reason. Those who find themselves in such a position will find benefits in contemplating such matters and applying just a small amount of logic and reason.

Problem-solving skills are essential for arriving at conclusions quickly and are rooted in our ability to use logic and reason. While other schools of thought focus on these concepts from an academic perspective, Stoicism is more inclined to emphasise their practical application. Therefore, if you study the concepts of logic and reason from a Stoic outlook, then you should remember to apply such learning with the same intention of practicality.

"For do you who can confer this freedom own no master? Have you no master in money, a girl lover, or a boy lover, the tyrant, or a friend of a tyrant? If not, why do you tremble when you go away to face a crisis of this sort? Therefore I say many times over: What you must practise and have at your command is to know what you ought to approach with confidence, and what with caution; all that is beyond the control of the will with confidence, and what is dependent on the will with caution."

—Epictetus

In other chapters we have discussed the concept of freeing ourselves from such masters as stated here by Epictetus. For unless we take action, we shall remain enslaved to them. Here, Epictetus confirms that our willpower plays a critical role in starting this process of becoming free, as the philosophers were themselves. The use of logic can aid us in this, if applied correctly towards these things that enslave us. It is certainly a worthy pursuit to have an internal dialogue with the use of logic to overcome these kinds of adversity.

Though if we are not confident or are hindered in some part by the things discussed within this chapter, we will not be able to deal with such problems at our fullest potential. Logic and reason, or at least the awareness of these concepts, can be the key to start breaking free from where we were previously stuck at those bridges that we need to cross.

This may be a good time to contemplate whether the concepts of logic and reason are suitable for you, as you are becoming more familiar with these concepts. Whilst doing so, also contemplate on Stoicism as a whole. Do you consider it something worthy of implementing in our lives? Is it a more practical philosophy as compared to the other schools of thought? What are the practicalities of implementing it in our lives? Will implementing this philosophy steer us towards becoming better versions of ourselves? With the use of logic, such questions can help us make an informed choice as to whether we wish to walk along the Stoic path.

"Just that you do the right thing. The rest does not matter."
—Marcus Aurelius

Once a person has ascended towards mastery of Stoicism, they would start to become a sage, which is a person who always has the ability to see the truth. This might have been merely an ideal that the Stoics pursued, rather than a practical reality. Becoming a sage is a journey that is never complete. The journey can come through solving simple or complex problems that might be presented from within or from an external source. Take strength from the journey itself, as you are always closer to this point of mastery than the one who never began to attempt such an undertaking.

This pursuit of the truth is a noble one. In the modern world, many people are susceptible to confirmation bias and make no attempt to work on this. If left unchecked, such a bias can hinder us from seeing the world for what it really is, instead seeing it for what we wish it to be.

So that their view of the world does not become clouded, in part or fully, the seeker of truth must continually fortify their mind. At times, this may require some or all of the concepts discussed within this book. The Stoics believed that only our impressions can lead us to the truth. On the contrary, modern epistemology is rather different in this regard, though discussing this further is outside the scope of this book.

The tools of logic can be applied to almost anything that one wishes. However, it would be prudent for us to use ours towards the higher end of what Stoicism is in pursuit of, as we have intended to set upon the path the Stoics presented us and should therefore exercise our faculties towards a similar goal. We should also use logic to analyse any premises presented to us by any and all schools of thought within the modern world in order to arrive at the same rationale as they saw and understand what they believed to be the highest good. As stated by Marcus Aurelius: "It is the truth I am after, for the truth did not harm anyone."

In the modern world, it is rare to see philosophers in action, doing what they do best. There are some debates online, but quite often it seems that the opposing sides are not willing to clearly articulate their positions, making it difficult for the other side to counter it. This kind of debating has in part lost its sincerity and has become more about winning or losing rather than arriving at the truth. Some of us may have observed or participated in debates within educational institutions or seen political debates on television. These, I would argue, are often more of a show rather than being grounded in clearly displayed philosophical positions.

For these kinds of reasons, a fair level of thought leadership will be required from those of us who intend to set upon the Stoic path in the modern world. The original Stoic teachers are not here with us, and not all of their works have survived to the present. Therefore, if we encounter situations in life that are not clearly addressed in the Stoic writings, then it will be up to us to piece together the knowledge we have gained and deal with any such matters accordingly. Additionally, we should strive to become independent in our understanding and application of Stoic principles, taking strength to walk this path alone without relying on anyone to continually check and correct us. The Stoic path is one that provides us with all the necessary tools to carry out the work needed within ourselves and in the external world.

"As fire tests gold, so misfortune tests brave men. See how high virtue must climb: you will learn the path she must take is fraught with peril:
'Steep is the way at first, which my steeds are scarce
Can climb in morning freshness; in mid sky
The altitude is greatest and the sight
Of land and sea has often struck
In my own heart an agony of fear.
The final part drops sheer; then above all
Control must be assured, and even she
Whose waters lie below to welcome me
Tethys, waits fearful lest I headlong fall.'
When he heard these words, that noble youth replied: 'I like the journey, I shall mount; though I fall, it is worth the risk to soar above such sights.'"

—Seneca

There are a couple of things we can take from such a discourse as quoted in Seneca's work. Firstly, this discourse shows how difficult it can be to pursue virtue. Secondly, we should see the courage of the youth, who is still willing to embark upon his journey after hearing what it entails. Although we were not present in the ancient world to witness such philosophical discourses firsthand, it is likely the philosophers would have been experts at unravelling their counterparts' arguments, which we would have been able to take great insights from. This is why I previously mentioned that thought leadership is required from us—we must become these inspirational philosophers ourselves.

The underlying reason that we often see flaws in people's reasoning when they engage in a discourse is perhaps that they lack a clear direction in their pursuit of truth. Confirmation bias, delusions and many other things can contribute to such a problem. As a result, the supporters of both sides of a debate are left unsatisfied, as the correct conclusion is never reached. The concepts of seeking the truth and also of *amor fati*, which involves accepting one's fate happily after trying one's best, are likely the missing wisdom in these situations.

It has not been my intention in this chapter to delve deep into the intricate details of Stoic logic and show how it compares with concepts of logic in other schools of thought. There are plenty of books that explore these very things, and the average person will not enjoy reading such works of scholarly depth. Instead, I have attempted to outline here the direction to the heights of wisdom the Stoics were in pursuit of, as logic and reason are the tools with which they were able to reach such heights.

I hope I have demonstrated the wisdom and practical utility of such things, that can be achieved quickly by even the average person who has not studied philosophy. We might take example from the noble youth described within the story outlined earlier from the works of Epictetus and say to ourselves something similar as the youth did before beginning his journey.

It should be mentioned here that the Stoics had a broader understanding of logic than it is commonly understood today, particularly regarding the inclusion of physics and ethics. This more comprehensive approach might work better for the average person as it provides tools that can be used to navigate a wider range of challenges.

Ethics is something we should be well grounded in, as it plays a significant role in building one's character. Ethics is intertwined through all of the concepts we are discussing throughout this book, as it deals with our inner worlds and how we should deal with the external world at the same time. Physics is also relevant to our Stoic journey, as it is concerned with the external world and nature, and living in accordance with nature is of central importance to the Stoic way of thought.

An old map of Italy where the Roman Senate was based within where Seneca and Marcus Aurelius held their positions.

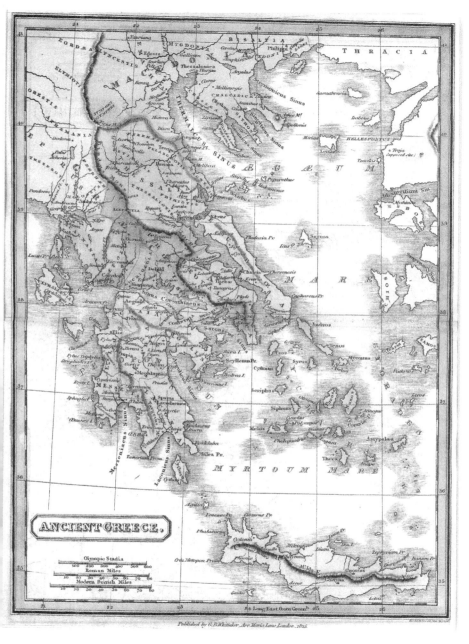

An old map of Greece in Agora of Athens where the Stoic
Philosophy originates during the Hellenistic period.

Looking at the External World

"Appearances to the mind are of four kinds. Things either are what they appear to be; or they neither are, nor appear to be; or they are, and do not appear to be; or they are not, and yet appear to be. Rightly to aim in all these cases is the wise man's task."

—Epictetus

In the above quote, Epictetus encourages us to look upon the external world with a view to figure out how and why things are as they appear to be and to recognise when things are not what they appear to be. If this examination is carried out correctly, then we shall attain the clarity that the wise man seeks to achieve and a deeper understanding of the external world. This is only possible after we have achieved clarity in our internal worlds by looking within to the self. It is important to maintain our focus and attention upon the external world, as the world is constantly changing. By increasing our critical thinking towards the external world, we will be able to put the principles of Stoicism into practice more effectively.

We can look into any works and recognise if they are coming from a place of benevolence and aligned towards virtue, which the Stoics placed as the highest good. Such a perspective is no longer commonplace, or something people actively think about in the modern world. These are not the messages relayed to us by the media, but by including virtue within our thoughts, we can make this world a better place.

By directing ourselves towards virtue, we will bring forth good towards humanity, which is an encouraging thought.

The journey we are all on will happen to us, so why not choose to happen to it? In this transient life, we will see the start of our journey and inevitably the end. What comes after is a matter of much debate. On this journey, we can do what society thinks is good, or we can independently choose to think in ways which are timelessly and universally good and bring about change to the best of our ability. The Stoic principles that lead us towards virtue have been tested far more by the passing of time than the modern ways of thought, which are ever-changing year after year.

When growing up, it is suggested to us that we should try to fit in with our peers, but if we look at the people we admire and respect, they are the ones who stand out, the ones who chose to separate from the pack. They saw that the world they were in had placed them on a trajectory that would not take them to the correct environment to achieve their goals. Thus, they took it upon themselves to do something different to get to somewhere different. They chose choice over chance, setting themselves upon what was most likely the harder path but the one that would lead to the greatest results.

The Stoics advise us to separate from the mob, even perhaps to join the ranks of the insane. The "ranks of the insane" is not to be understood literally. Rather, it simply means that it does not matter what others think of us or how at times our path may even seem to us along the way.

The major religions of the world, as well as the Stoics, have emphasised that life is transient. Despite how much focus the ancients gave this thought, it appears that people in the modern world are not so inclined to reflect on such a matter. One reason for this may be the advancement of science that had a part to play, as an increase in technology has led to more creation of material goods, providing people with more distractions. While the scientific method is good for what it can be used for, which is to observe nature and its workings, it may not be appropriate to use it to answer questions about the nature of the metaphysical and supernatural worlds. Another reason for the lack of reflection may be that people living in certain geographical locations may reject the dominant religion if, after examining it with logic and rationale, found it to be illogical or inconsistent, and concluded that atheism was more suited to them. However, this does not mean that other religions or belief systems should be disregarded without consideration. Just as in academia, we should examine all sources of information on a particular subject and not reject some due to them being from unfamiliar places.

If we skip over the fundamental premises of our wisdom and instead try to start further down the road, then how do we know that what we've found is really the truth? It would be correct to say that we do not truly know until the final hour, when it's all on the line. The pursuit of knowledge can be looked upon like any competition we engage in. The victory is not won or lost in the actual event but rather in the countless hours of training.

The Stoics believed that after we have made good progress in our inner battle with the self, we can strive to bring about positive change in the external world. We can be inspired by this to do the same as the Stoics and work towards making the world a better place, guided by the principles of Stoicism, which are likely to be agreeable to all who explore them.

We shall certainly encounter adversity along the way when attempting to work on any such change, and it is useful to think of these adversities as obstacles, not limits. If we stay positive and believe we can overcome these obstacles, then we can get past them to bring about the results we desire.

At this point, let's bring our attention to the business world. There are many factors that contribute to success in this field, and many of these require the wisdom and ability to see the external world for how it really is. If we do not correctly see the business landscape in which we operate, then any actions we take within it will also be incorrect and lead our business along the wrong path. When many decisions require a risk to be taken, how do we make the correct decisions and know which risks to take?

This requires foresight and seeing the world correctly. This clarity helps to ensure you do not miss important information and are not misinformed when taking risks. Your perspective and your perception of what is in front of you will determine whether you succeed or fail. Those who have worked on their inner selves will then have the required clarity and will not be looking at the world through a particular lens that obscures the view.

The principles of Stoicism are presented with utility and practicality in mind, and they should be combined with our existing wisdom to provide us with a firm grounding, enabling us to move forward and make decisions confidently and correctly, thus enhancing our leadership qualities and allowing us to direct our organisations towards the success we desire.

This clarity is also needed due to the fast pace of change in the modern world. It is necessary for business leaders to know what things are worth taking note of and what is simply noise to ignore as it will have no impact on the organisation. They must take action on that which is relevant, all the while keeping in mind the principles of Stoicism and remaining along the path towards virtue.

It is important to take counsel from others, but carefully choose from whom this is taken. This is a task in its own right and should be carried out before counsel is required, so that going forward, your trusted sources can be utilised as situations arise.

Further wisdom is then required to either act upon or reject any such advice that has been presented. It is a common trait of leaders to seek counsel and the same was rightly so for the Stoics, as shown in the following dialogue between Hadrian and Epictetus.

"Hadrian. *What is gold?*
Epictetus. *A servant of death.*
Hadrian. *What is silver?*
Epictetus. *The seat of envy.*
Hadrian. *What is iron?*
Epictetus. *The instrument of all arts.*
Hadrian. *What is a sword?*
Epictetus. *The law of camps.*
Hadrian. *What is a gladiator?*
Epictetus. *A lawful homicide.*
Hadrian. *What people in good health are yet sick?*
Epictetus. *Those who meddle with other people's business.*
Hadrian. *What is a man never tired of?*
Epictetus. *Of making money.*
Hadrian. *What is liberty?*
Epictetus. *Innocence.*
Hadrian. *What is common to all kings and miserable men?*
Epictetus. *To be born and to die.*
Hadrian. *What is best and worst?*
Epictetus. *Words.*
Hadrian. *What is man?*
Epictetus. *He is like a lamp or candle set in the wind.*
Hadrian. *What is love?*
Epictetus. *The trouble of a peaceful breast; modesty or shame in a boy; blushes in a girl; a fury in a woman; ardour in a young man; a joke in old age; a crime in a seducer.*
Hadrian. *What is God?*
Epictetus. *He who holds all things in His hands.*"

This quaint dialogue was recorded in the manuscript, the *Altercatio Hadriani Augusti et Epicteti Philopsophi*, with 65 such questions posed by Hadrian.

Though the dialogue as presented is fictitious, we can still draw wisdom from it. Although there is not much chance we shall have someone of Epictetus' calibre from whom we can seek such counsel, we should likewise find some even-minded people we can trust to advise us, as the Stoics considered even-mindedness to be the greatest virtue. The quoted dialogue seems to take place in a leisurely setting. The questions are quite general, encompassing a broad spectrum of things. When we require counsel ourselves, we are more likely to seek advice regarding a particular situation, mostly due to the fast pace of the modern world.

When we attempt to look upon the external world to see it for what it is, there is always a chance that, for whatever reason, some details escape our sight. A good reason to take counsel is to gain further insight or another perspective on a situation, which might alert us to those details we overlooked.

Finding an appropriate mentor to guide us along our journey, as both Hadrian and Marcus Aurelius did, is a very useful thing that should not be underestimated. The utility of such guidance will surely be of much benefit to us.

When engaging in critical thinking, it is important to structure the process by first ensuring the underlying principles of our question are valid and applicable to the subject at hand. This allows us to reach a conclusion that is driven by the underlying principles throughout the process from start to completion. This structured thinking is part of the workings of the inner world, but the action taken once these conclusions are reached becomes a part of the external world. The process of critical thinking has ensured that our actions in the external world are built on solid foundations, even when faced with adversity. We will have already instilled in ourselves the mental toughness and fortitude necessary to overcome any such obstacle.

"You must plan your life, one action at a time, and be content if each acquires its own end as best it can; and that it should acquire its end, no one at all can prevent you. 'But some external obstacle will be in the way.' None to prevent action with justice, temperance and due reflection. 'But possible some other activity will be hindered.' Still, by meeting the actual obstacle with resignation and good-temperedly altering your course to what is granted you, a new action is at once substituted, which will fit into the plan of which we are speaking."
—Marcus Aurelius

This statement by Marcus Aurelius can be understood from the perspective of looking at the world and seeing it for what it is. Here, he advises that we should keep focused on our goal even when we discover that the path towards it isn't going in a straight line. In such a scenario, we should keep focused and embody the qualities mentioned within the above statement. Even when faced with obstacles, you should not turn back, but instead navigate around them, by sidestepping, climbing over them or taking any such necessary action to carry on in our initial direction. These obstacles are only temporary.

But what is there to gain from doing this and maintaining this course of direction? Well, this will strengthen your character and bring you to new heights that you never thought possible. Think of it like a present wrapped in layers of wrapping paper. Each layer of wrapping paper is a new adversity, but after each layer, you get closer to the present. Once all the layers have been removed, then you have your present: newfound skills that will last the test of time and prove useful again and again. This new strength of character will enable you to look towards new goals and take you along the path of mastery that you set out to walk.

There are two kinds of obstacles: those that emerge from the inner self and those that exist in the physical world. The art of recognising which of the two you are facing is important to learn. You will need to judge these obstacles correctly at first glance so that internal obstacles do not set in and become bigger obstacles than they need to be. For example, fear is always something that should be dealt with soon as it arrives, because if it sets in then it will hinder your actions going forward in any regard. However, if the fear is in response to an actual external danger that we should make ourselves safe from, then we should listen to such an emotion as it is there to protect us. In most other cases, it is merely something to overcome so we can reach the next level of our personal growth.

Obstacles will present themselves throughout any journey, and how we face them will inevitably be a deciding factor in how we build our character. If we seek to build our character, then it becomes our duty to anticipate and deal with these obstacles accordingly. Any such obstacles that are part of the external world we should meet and see for what they truly are. The overcoming of these adversities will demonstrate how Stoic principles can be applied in real-time to various situations.

The more adversities we overcome, the more our wisdom will increase. As long as our actions are grounded in underlying Stoic principles, then we need not pay so much attention to what the majority thinks. We have already chosen a path where resistance is expected as part of the journey.

How does one on the Stoic path also survive and thrive within the modern world of phoniness? Well, we must cultivate the quality of even-mindedness, which is needed now more than it ever was for the Stoics. Short-term thinking pervades our culture, but we must pay attention to the long term. The Stoics thought long-term and won the decade not the day.

Put your principles into practice and find your strengths. Do not follow the herd like sheep, never looking further ahead than the one in front of you. It is the duty of the wise man to find his own path and continually re-examine this path, as it can be quite easy to get distracted, especially in the modern world. As thought by Epictetus, every small milestone you pass should be celebrated. As the journey is not an easy one, this can be a good practice to keep yourself encouraged.

Each individual will face adversities unique to them. Overcoming these obstacles correctly will aid with the personal growth necessary to bring about change within the external world, which others will respect once they have seen it. However, it is common for these efforts to be discouraged or even mocked until success is achieved. As the Stoics recommended, when faced with such resistance, you should be strict with yourself and tolerant with others. We can add a further saying from Marcus Aurelius: "The impediment to action advances action. What stands in the way becomes the way."

Every action starts with a thought, therefore our actions should be guided from their inception to their outcome by Stoic principles directed towards virtue. These are especially needed in the modern age, and it is my intention to make them popular once again. This book is my way of sharing something that has brought me character growth and helped me overcome adversities along my own path. As I looked upon the external world, I saw some things within it that are not in agreement with nature and the universal good, so I set about increasing my knowledge of Stoicism, and whilst doing so, I acquired more tools to align my thoughts with a more grounded outlook. I hope all those who read this book will achieve similar results as I did.

This brings our attention to the new technological tools available to us and whether they are truly assisting us towards the betterment of ourselves. While this does depend on how we use them, we should also understand the intentions of those who created such things in the first place. Only then from this starting point can we utilise these tools correctly. Let's take social media as an example. It has gained popularity at great speed without anyone questioning the outcomes of making it a part of our lives. Certainly, a lot of people and businesses have benefitted from it. However, the intentions of the makers of such apps are clearly for us all to spend as much time as possible on these things. Therefore, we should step back, consider this and ask ourselves if we are spending too much time on these apps.

Then the second thing to ask ourselves would be whether these things are actually of benefit to us. This question is important because we need to make sure we are spending our time only on beneficial pursuits such as one's self growth. We all only have 24 hours in the day, and we should spend them wisely.

The slogans and catchphrases prevalent on social media can lead to people adopting ways of thinking that sound good at the time. People will quickly come to hold on to these thoughts, thinking they are their own thoughts, but they did not actually formulate these by themselves and often have no idea what philosophy or opinion and background this particular thought came from. By absorbing information in such a way without the study of philosophy, logic and reason, individuals will most certainly become the victims of being only half informed on any particular subject.

Therefore, we can see that while social media can be used for our benefit, only a few will truly do this. The majority will quite simply waste time using these tools without much real benefit, when they could have spent that time on pursuits of much greater value.

How these tools are thought of and utilised could even be an example of the obstacles we have been discussing.

So, we can view overcoming this as just another task of a wise man.

It is possible to hone a mindset in which you can quickly analyse the truth. As noted in Malcolm Gladwell's book *Blink*, after attaining a certain level of expertise in discerning the truth, it is possible for our intuition to provide us with instant answers to any obstacle we face. We can call this fight or flight, intuition, a sixth sense, a flow state, or many other names. It can be easier to achieve such a state if we fine-tune the smaller skills that hover subtly around the core Stoic principles and skill sets, which can lead to quite extraordinary results when combined.

"Hang on to your youthful enthusiasms—you'll be able to use them better when you're older."

—Seneca

This quote by Seneca can be a powerful motivator if thought about correctly. In our youth, we all possess enthusiasm, but it is quite raw and unadulterated. We have not yet faced the tolls of society telling us we cannot do things and must fit in with our peers. In our days of maturity, once these tolls have set in, we may not have as much enthusiasm left in the tank. However, we will have more wisdom and a clearer idea of the path we wish to traverse. Holding on to or renewing our youthful enthusiasm will serve us far better at this stage of our lives.

We must maintain clarity regarding the path we are walking, guided by the Stoic principles, all the while staying motivated and maintaining enthusiasm to walk through the mud to get to the higher ground. This will make the journey more worthwhile and fruitful, as it will seem less arduous and ultimately become more enjoyable as each adversity is overcome. By doing so, we will further fine-tune ourselves and uncover greater levels of skill within ourselves that are needed to achieve more and travel further, always driven by the unrelenting purpose of reaching our goal. Excellence does not care about your feelings; it only cares about results. Therefore, enthusiasm will serve us greatly along the way.

We should be aware of our own cognitive biases and continually reevaluating the things we believe we know. Certain Stoic principles will work in some situations but not others. For example, it is important to reciprocate respect with those who genuinely show it, but not with those who only fake it. Fake respect is only used by those who are seeking something from you, or who are people-pleasers, in which case their agreeability is unlikely to come from a place of integrity. In the worst-case scenario, an enemy can present fake respect to mislead you into something that is fully in their interests and not yours. Therefore, it is important to discern the difference between situations that on the face of these things appear similar, and act accordingly.

The pursuit of objective truth should be sought with the intention of seeing through the barrage of noise and smoke and mirrors the external world presents. It is important to understand and accept that both the inner self and the external world are quite complex in nature. This acceptance will bring forth the resilience to progress on the path towards clarity of vision, which will allow us to see obstacles that perhaps may have originally been hidden.

This brings our attention to the importance of having foresight in order to predict obstacles before they appear. Through careful planning, you can clear the path before embarking upon it, and anticipate its twists and turns. Though we can only connect the dots when looking back and not ahead, as the dots that lie ahead have not yet been seen, through hindsight we can try and predict the pattern ahead.

"If you ever come on a dense wood of ancient trees that have risen to an exceptional height, shutting out all sight of the sky with one thick screen of branches upon another, the loftiness of the forest, the seclusion of the spot, your sense of wonderment at finding so deep and unbroken a gloom out of doors, will persuade you of the presence of a deity. Any cave in which the rocks have been eroded deep into the mountain resting on it, its hollowing out into a cavern of impressive extent not produced by the labours of men but the result of processes of nature, will strike your soul some kind of inkling of the divine."

—Seneca

What Seneca is touching upon here is our innate disposition to, at times when we gaze upon things of such magnificence, become ignited with notions of the divine, of a higher power that designed these things. I, for one, can relate to this as I have felt such things when being present within the vastness and power of nature. I can further relate to this, as throughout the Quran, the reader is asked to look upon the signs of their Lord so as to create awareness of such things. Seneca apparently carried out such a task and it pointed him towards a certain direction, although he would not have ever come across the Quran, as he was around during a similar time to Jesus (PBUH).

When you see such greatness in nature, no one thinks: "Wow—what a big bang it must have been to bring all this into existence!" It seems we are programmed to some extent to see divinity in such things. This inherent conditioning persists, even in the modern world, where science and modernity would have conditioned us all to perhaps think the opposite—after all, they do have the school curriculum and the media on their side. My personal opinion is that I would agree with Seneca on this matter: such places persuade you of the presence of a deity.

Then this brings our attention to the relevance of this in the modern world for us to think about. Certainty on such matters of religion would need much knowledge. Even with all the modern technological advancements available to us, the debates on these topics still continue. Some believe that science will one day have all the answers, while others acknowledge science's usefulness but realise that each thing has its place and the scientific method may not ever be able to fully test or explain certain phenomena. It would be wise, then, to take the knowledge and wisdom gained from the sciences, while also incorporating philosophical logic and reasoning to better understand the objective truth of these matters.

"You have sent me a letter by the hand of a 'friend' of yours, as you call him. And in the next sentence you warn me to avoid discussing your affairs freely with him, since you are not even in the habit of doing so yourself; in other words you have described him as being a friend and then denied this in one and the same letter. Now if you were using that word in a kind of popular sense and not according to its strict meaning, and calling him a 'friend' in much the same way as we refer candidates as 'gentlemen' or hail someone with the greeting 'my dear fellow' if when we meet him his name slips our memory, we can let this pass. But if you are looking on anyone as a friend when you do not trust him as you trust yourself, you are making a grave mistake and have failed to grasp sufficiently the full force of true friendship."

—Seneca

Understanding our interactions with other people and the potential benefit or harm they pose to us is a crucial part of judging the external world correctly. The Stoic principles will serve us well to assist with these matters.

In Seneca's letter above, he discusses the ambiguous use of the word "friend" and why such a term would be used in this manner. Even minor issues such as this can be of concern depending on the situation, and we may face similar uncertainty about such things, as well as bigger matters related to the divine realities. It is important to approach all such matters with an open mind, as our perception of truth may have been influenced by external conditioning. Pursuing these matters with an even mind is a thing of virtue in itself. I wish all who read this book the best of luck on the journey to discovering the truth of such things.

Quite aptly here, another statement by Seneca is fitting:

"I view with pleasure and approval the way you keep on at your studies and sacrifice everything to your single-minded efforts to make yourself every day a better man. I do not merely urge you to persevere in this; I actually implore you to. Let me give you, though, this one piece of advice: refrain from following the example of those whose craving is for attention, not their own improvement, by doing certain things which are calculated to give rise to comment on your appearance or way of living generally. Avoid shabby attire, long hair, an unkempt beard, an outspoken dislike of silverware, sleeping on the ground and all other misguided means to self-advertisement. The very name of philosophy, however modest the manner in it is pursued, is unpopular enough as it is; imagine what the reaction would be if we started dissociating ourselves from the conventions of society. Inwardly everything should be different but our outward face should conform with the crowd."

—Seneca

We have established that it is worthwhile to pursue looking at the external world. Achieving the results we desire will take a combination of inner personal growth and a more in-depth understanding of the external world. Doing so will inevitably bring a kind of success not experienced by the majority. The Stoic principles of wisdom, courage, self-control and justice should be the tools we work with to help us gain the deeper understanding of objective reality.

We obtain this understanding now so we will never have to wonder what could have been if we had seen our endeavours through to the end. Often, we'll make New

Year's resolutions that start off well. After a couple of months, once the grind of things has started to break us down, those resolutions are gone with the wind till next year, leaving us with a question: *what if?* What if we'd kept up the resolution? What would the results look and feel like? Well, if we just had the grit to keep at it, then we would already have the results and any resolutions we made thereafter would be to further us towards new levels of progression. So perhaps the best thing is not to wait for New Year's Eve or any other date. Just start immediately. You need a "right now, right here" kind of attitude. We don't need the external world to provide us with perfect settings, and we do not need to be fully motivated and feeling good to start things. Rather, we should just start and figure things out along the way. The more work we put in, the greater the results and the luckier we become, as our wisdom will always increase along the way as well.

Achieving our goals will require strength of character. Those who prioritise pleasure above all else will gain little from strengthening their character, as at any time they may surrender to their whims and desires and indulge in the things they want. For those who understand that achieving anything worth striving for will definitely require sacrifice and grit to last the distance, no matter how difficult things get and no matter how much we do not want to continue with the journey, working on the inner self is crucial. We must get the correct mindset right at the start of the journey, as it is the thing we are going to reference back to when the going gets tough. It will serve as a guiding light in the dark times, and act as the fuel to help us take that one step forward when we have nothing else left in the tank.

We enjoy inspirational stories and movies that provide a feeling of motivation, but they only motivate us within comfortable surroundings at our leisure. Why do we not provide this motivation for ourselves? Sometimes we can look behind us and see all that we have achieved, the adversities we have overcome, and realise just how far we've come. Looking at what we may achieve further along the path makes us feel like heroes. We do not need some other hero to look at. The lessons we learnt and the wisdom we acquired will always be with us to be used when any other challenges present themselves.

You should remain open to any improvements, as even the smallest change can be seen as a stepping stone to make reaching the next milestone just that bit easier. These small nuances are the very things that separate the "good enough" from the professionals.

One thing that is certain is that the external world is always changing. The wise thing to do is to be malleable enough to keep up and thrive within this environment, while never forgetting the principles that we chose to carry with us before setting upon this path. By keeping an eye out for those changes that will impact us, we will also remain tuned in to the impact we can make on the external world for the better.

But what exactly is the betterment we seek to bring to the external world? This will most definitely vary from person to person, as each individual will have formulated their own findings from the work they have carried out in the realm of the inner self and will have a different sense of the betterment they can bring. Whatever our goal, we shall come across many along the way who have been conditioned by society and have not necessarily undergone the journey of looking within to find strength and build their character. Such people may very well then present resistance against the betterment we seek to bring forth. In this clash of ideas, there are a number of ways in which you can challenge this kind of adversity.

We live in the information age and not the age of the sword, so the first thing to acquire in such a conflict is a sound knowledge of the subjects that we are engaging with. This will grant us a sound rationale by which we can engage with any interlocutor. The second thing is to ensure that we do not allow ourselves to be led to a place where we are triggered by our emotions.

"Stoicism is about the domestication of our emotions, not their elimination."

—Nasim Nicholas Taleb

The above advice is something we can take forward with us into public debates or even meetings at work, in which the other side might try to incite some kind of emotional response from us that, if brought out, would weaken our position within the discussion. Some of you may have heard examples of this when listening to a discussion on the radio when a caller calls in. Even if their opinion is correct, the host challenging their views can bring out such an emotional response that it weakens their position, perhaps even to the point where their argument just seems like nonsense to the listening audience. As an opposite example, you might have seen a leading politician be interviewed on the television and remain calm by simply skimming past a difficult point in its entirety. This is equally unadvisable, as many people would see how the politician simply ignores the point. By instead applying Stoic principles and sound rationale we would hopefully have no need to use such an avoidance technique. However, we can still learn from this example that it is up to us whether we allow whomever we engage with to trigger an emotional response within us. The Stoics have said that whoever angers an individual then becomes his master.

If we look around the external world regarding relationships with each other, what do we find? Well, as statistics show, divorce rates have gone through the roof in all parts of the world and in all types of communities. Focus has shifted from the community to the individual. Conflict between men and women is pushed online and into the media, or between the left and the right, or basically everyone vs everyone in some form or another. Could a lack of popular interest in philosophy be a contributing factor to these frictions? The majority have hardly any understanding of this subject. In our major cities, we do not find prominent philosophers such as the Stoics, whose gatherings we could attend to listen to. In ancient times, philosophy must have gotten quite a lot of traction through such forums. For example, when the Islamic empire came across the Greek philosophies, these started to gather quite some momentum therein. Prominent thinkers like Al Ghazali, Ibn Sina and Ibn Taymiyyah dealt with these philosophies through the lenses of their own philosophies, which were and still are grounded in Islam.

At times, humans find utility in something profound and keep it with them, but at other times they will slowly let go of things which were good for them. Sometimes, the victors of the times will present the message that such-and-such caused such a thing, and if this is repeated enough times then this is what gets remembered. Again we can see the wisdom in leaving the opinion of the masses and joining the ranks of the insane, for even when faced with the statistics, the masses will tell the wise man that he is insane to hold a different view from them. For these masses, who enjoy all that the modern world has to offer, may fear that if they disagree with the messages they have been told, they may be shunned and lose these perks they have been enjoying. The choice here is to see things as they are, as the Stoics recommended, or to see the external world for what you wish it to be.

This same choice is offered to the character Neo in the *Matrix* movie, in the form of the red and the blue pill.

The Stoics would have chosen the red pill, choosing to see things as they really are, though it seems the majority in ancient times as well as in the present day do otherwise and take the blue pill, continuing to see things as they wish for them to be.

For how can we correctly follow virtue if our search is based not on how the external world is but rather as we wish to see it? If our perspective is flawed, the nature in which we follow virtue is then also flawed. The truth is the truth; it cannot be changed, and things are as they are. The issue, then, is with our vision and understanding, not the actual things themselves. For the very thing that we seek—virtue—is correct, as is the seeking, but we have hindered ourselves in attaining it as what we think it is is in fact something else entirely.

So then it really is a wise man's task to look and look again at what the external world really is in order to do what is right and lead us towards the aims of virtue in accordance with nature.

Why is it that divorce rates are so high? Why are so many segments of society pitted against one another? Well, for one, we have yet to see the full outcome of the implementation of postmodern ideals. These have not yet stood the test of time. It is also questionable whether technology is making us better people. How many times do we see people talking to each other online in ways that they would not in person? This could be due to there being no repercussions, as they are not in the same physical space as each other. Or it could simply be that this is how we are. Either way, it does not look good to the audience.

The point being that the diminishing of ancient philosophies and religious ethics as compared to modern ideals may not be a good thing. While on the surface it may seem to be, looking just a bit deeper may show us otherwise. Either way, here we can see the importance of seeing things as they are.

"There are three departments in which a man who is to be good and noble must be trained. The first concerns the will to get and will to avoid; he must be trained not to fail to get what he wills to get nor fall into what he wills to avoid. The second is concerned with impulse to act and not to act, and, in a word, the sphere of what is fitting: that we should act in order, with due consideration, and with proper care. The object of the third is that we may not be deceived, and may not judge at random, and generally it is concerned with assent."

—Epictetus

Quite frequently, we see the Stoics use the term "ascent" in regard to ascending towards objectivity. Similarly, the term "random" is often used in a negative light and is considered something to avoid. Combining these ideas, it is essential to not begin an ascent in a random direction, whether this be in dealing with our inclinations, in discussions with others or in our actions. We should strive to be noble, which is a good thing, though a term that is not often used in the modern day. Whilst having this as part of our character, we should undergo training to exercise our will with logic and rationale, whilst our ascent should always be towards virtue. We can only gain momentum in this ascent if we rightly know when to pursue an impulse and when to avoid it completely. Impulses can come from within us quite spontaneously or can be deliberately incited by others. Either way, it is important for us to control our emotions, as they can cause us to think or act out of character, and possibly then to ascend in the wrong direction. Avoiding deception is certainly a wise man's task. We have already covered deception in one sense, regarding the fallacies of the masses, but it can also occur between individuals. To avoid finding ourselves in such a position, we should use our faculties to the fullest with all that our wisdom has taught us, the sound principles that we hold, and the structured way that we think. We should especially avoid leaving gaps within our reasoning, for if we do then those very gaps will become the doors by which others will find the openings to mislead us entirely. We will be led in the wrong direction, all the while thinking it is the correct one. If instead we maintain our intent toward ascent, then it will provide us with sufficient reasoning to avoid creating any such gaps.

When a person on this ascent looks back at their journey, they can see that they are reaching new, higher levels. Once this has been seen enough times, then it becomes a proven practice, not just a theory. So then the question arises: why can this Stoic outlook not be used for as many things as possible? It surely can indeed.

Another thing to consider here is whether modern technology is helping us to embody Stoic virtues, or if it is hindering progress on our ascent. Media, and specifically social media, is by design there to absorb our time by providing us entertainment which is very addictive. They have the capability to provide us with instant fame, but in the background, many such things are collecting information about us that we may not be looking to provide until they know us in ways in which perhaps we may not even know ourselves, all for the sake of personalisation. Stoic philosophy requires much thought and a great attention span, but some of these new technologies deliberately lessen our attention spans with short clips of entertainment. There are many aspects of the external world that should be considered carefully—far more than I can cover within this book—but this particular example is a prudent one for us to look at closely as it has much potential to hinder us along our journey.

Knowing the effects that such technologies have on us, are we really living in accordance with nature by indulging in use of such technology on a daily basis? Back in the day, when we were hunter-gatherers, would we have spent our time sitting in one place with a small item in our hands, with the attention span of a goldfish? What about in the age of the philosophers? Quite simply the answer to both is no. And if we are not living in accordance with nature then it is the wise man's task to identify the thing that is hindering us from travelling along our path.

"Are we to say then that in this sphere alone, the greatest and most momentous of all, the sphere of freedom, it is permitted me to indulge chance desires? By no means: education is just this—learning to frame one's will in accord with events."

—Epictetus

I may be inserting more quotes into this chapter than strictly necessary, but the theme of this chapter is a central one within Stoic philosophy, and therefore, I am aiming to present a vast wealth of Stoic wisdom that readers can take from this chapter. This chapter is also very much interlinked with all the other chapters. For if it is the intention of the Stoics to provide us with freedom, then we must be able to identify when anything the external world presents us with is not aligned with this concept. If we do not consider such things, then no matter how much work we put in on our path, there will be some vices in the background that slow us down. If we recognise these hindrances for what they are and act accordingly to remove this weight, we can swiftly progress on our journey.

This brings our attention to the Stoic claim that only the educated are free. While they were referring to education within the schools of thought, we can still apply this wisdom today, even though we do not have these same teachers with us. It's important to contextualise their teachings in the present day and use these concepts to tackle the challenges we face in the external world today, as these challenges were not so present when the Stoics were teaching.

We have already mentioned how we must be a student in order to reach mastery, and then once again become the student. This time, our version of the student will have many tools that we did not at the start of our journey. The reasoning for this is that the master is often not malleable, whilst the student remains flexible. We should strive to master the Stoic concepts that are relevant to us or that we can incorporate into use in a modern context. These concepts will need to be applied to deal with certain challenges that were not present in ancient times, so we may be alone upon this part of the journey, as it seems to be an unbeaten path.

My aim within this chapter has been to provide you with insight into where you began this journey, where you will be after understanding the Stoic teachings, and then where you will be equipped to go with the tools provided by the Stoics on your individual journey.

The Stoic Path Alone?

Stoicism used to be a prevalent philosophy, but it has lost its fame over the years. However, it has seen a recent reemergence in modern times. Those of us who choose to set out upon the Stoic path must remain steadfast towards its goal, without faltering or being swayed towards other directions. It is wise to remain solely focused on a singular objective: the ascent towards building character by applying all that is discussed within this book. One who has chosen to walk the Stoic path should not mix concepts and principles from ancient or modern schools of thought with Stoicism, as these can provide contrary positions. For example, Stoicism and Epicureanism lead in different directions and to different destinations, these being pleasure for the Epicureans and virtue for the Stoics.

By attempting to follow two paths at the same time, we can easily develop contradictions within our understanding. Just as one would not merge two different religions together, the same applies to philosophy. Such a combination likely leads to us faltering on our path, as we have not done the work to identify and understand that these philosophies are built on differing premises that lead to different conclusions, and yet we attempt to travel in both directions at the same time, remaining confused, perhaps only looking at the surface of things. Sometimes we may find similarities between different schools of thought; however, those who are at the start of their journey should use caution in this regard.

To reach our desired destination, it is important to discern where we are starting from and where we are looking to get to. If the road map and framework have been given to us by a particular school of thought, then we should work out if this is the correct path in the first instance. In the modern world, it is often presented that all paths are correct and all directions are the right ones, but we should discern whether this truly is the case. By ensuring our path is the correct one, we will save time and effort in the long run. Confusion is the beginning of learning, but once we have overcome it and gained clarity, we should not risk returning to confusion by deviating from our chosen path through the inclusion of other philosophical ideas from outside the realms of Stoicism.

From the outset, the Stoic philosophy offers clear insights, and going further into the details of it will only provide more of the same. Thus, in our initial stages of learning, there is really not much utility to be found in the inclusion of other ideas from different schools of thought. However, for those who are more advanced or are within the realms of academia, then such things are fine, as they are being carried out for completely different reasons than self-improvement. From an academic point of view, we can compare the outlook of different schools of thought to that of Stoicism at our discretion. Once we have mastered the concepts of Stoicism, we can more easily recognise when different ideas we are presented with are compatible with Stoicism. In general, though, the Stoic way is sufficient and does not need additional input from external sources of philosophy, whether they are competing or non-competing.

"For I am not everlasting, but a human being, a part of the whole as an hour is a part of the day, and like an hour I must pass away."
—Epictetus

The Stoics remind us time and again that this life is transient and we are merely passing through on this short journey. It is important to consider the value and deeper meaning of this information. It's unrealistic to expect, with our limited time, that we can reach mastery in all areas of knowledge and schools of thought. Keeping this in mind, it would be prudent not to try, and instead, with wisdom, choose the path that is best suited to us. Such a decision will test our biases and let us use rationality, humility and foresight to decide if the Stoic path really is the best for us. Perhaps these reminders of our limited time are frequently mentioned by the Stoics, as comparably this path is much less to do with the academic realm. Instead, to those who choose to pursue it, this path offers the practical tools to overcome any adversity.

If we look at the positions of other schools of thought regarding similar concepts to those of the Stoics, we will find much of the same kind of differences. Looking at all such schools in detail would be a long journey. If you have already chosen a path, you will have no use for such a comparison.

I will present a few questions here in order to remain even-minded with regard to the Stoic framework, for the purposes of seeing if what this school offers is coherent. Can the ideas of this school withstand the onslaught of logic and reason? Do the ideas of the Stoics form a cohesive whole? Do all their teachings lead unfalteringly to virtue? By examining Stoicism through a critical lens, we can determine the strength of its foundations, particularly with regard to virtue and character building. It is the aim of this book to equip you with the tools necessary to discern these things for yourself. Once these Stoic positions in regard to mindset, outlook, principles and the ability to use the Stoic concepts have been found, the benefits will instantly be seen and the aforementioned questions will be answered. You will have taken what you have learnt, applied it in real situations and seen how these ideas have assisted you in overcoming adversity, thus proving that this school is built on solid foundations and its ideas have practical use in reality.

In the modern world, we have the understanding and the tools to answer such questions through practical application of the wisdom attained. We can apply this wisdom in real time to ourselves and the external world around us. We can even contemplate these questions by observing what we see in the media, news or online, without necessarily undertaking extensive research.

"If anyone can refute me—show me I'm making a mistake or looking at things from the wrong perspective—I'll gladly change. It is the truth I'm after. And the truth never harmed anyone."
—Marcus Aurelius

This quote refers to the importance of being even-minded, for anyone can make a mistake. If you realise that you have, then you should not double down and cling to this fault. We are not perfect, and any number of things could have led to the complete truth escaping us—perhaps our initial impressions, our emotions or the fact that we did not have all the details of a particular matter. However, once we have more wisdom, we can bring such a flaw back under our control, and if it is not serving us well, we can remove it from ourselves accordingly. For if we should fall into this error, then we are also failing to see the world for what it really is and not for what we wish it to be.

The modern world presents us with many ideas and simultaneously the lack thereof. Many of these ideas have not been tested with time, or lack critical thinking and logic. In comparison, the Stoic path has been travelled by some of history's wisest figures, who have reached great heights with this philosophy. Stoicism also embraces more advanced concepts such as metaphysics, ontology and epistemology, which are of use to those who would like to further their understanding of the philosophy or enter academic realms to battle other philosophical schools.

The modern world asserts that its ideas, born of experience and evolution, are superior to those of the ancients, and leads us to think that, especially in the fields of science and technology, we should follow their leadership. However, when it comes to ancient philosophy, we are not even aware of how many thousands of years it took to develop these ideas, while modern philosophy spans only a couple of hundred years. Comparing modern ways of thought to those of the ancients should be done with a level of humility. Further to this, if we compare the actual philosophers of the modern and the ancient worlds, it becomes evident which of these had greater depth of knowledge. While this judgement may be somewhat subjective, we can safely say that the philosophers of the ancient world were most certainly the giants whose foundations their modern counterparts have built upon.

The modern world has seen many instances where thinkers have gone in a completely wrong direction. In the realms of technology, it may seem as though it is a fine approach to break all barriers to attain the goals of such pursuits. However, from the perspective of philosophy, morality and ethics, this may not necessarily be the best approach. This is why any school of thought should be tested with time. However, as the masses do not tend to show an interest in philosophy, it becomes easier for ideas to become popular swiftly without much opposition.

Stoicism presents to us the idea that we should be virtuous to humanity in general, and not simply within our nation. To be virtuous means to be perfectly rational and to know both how to act in private and with respect to one's friends, business, associates, fellow citizens or countrymen, or indeed other members of the human race, as noted by Seneca.

The Stoic way of thought is sound for it is focused on the individual and the inner self. It is crucial to begin the journey by first looking inward and working on building our character and principles. Once we have established a strong inner foundation, we can begin to look to the external world and our conduct therein, with the goal of cultivating virtue. This virtuous behaviour is to be presented to all humanity and not only to our countrymen. Throughout Stoic literature, there is a strong emphasis on the self as opposed to relations with others. The wisdom we can take from this is that if we cultivate our inner world correctly, to attain high character while remaining directed by virtue, then we shall act with righteousness and in accordance with nature, which we are all a part of.

If the Stoic teachers had been around during the Industrial Revolution, then they would likely have opposed the technological advancements that have brought much benefit to humanity yet also caused much damage to the environment. The Stoics most definitely would have championed causes that resisted such developments. In today's world, where rainforests are being cut down and plastic waste is just about everywhere, we can see that those driving such technological advancements have not been inclined to minimise environmental damage and pursue environmentally friendly alternatives, which we have only started to do in recent years. If instead we interpret "living in accordance with nature" as referring to living according to the highest aspects of our rationale, then by this understanding too we can see that these masters of logic would have had quite something to say about the damage humanity has done to nature. Stoic thinking has always protected nature and held it in high esteem, while the modern world has only recently begun to take this issue seriously. Therefore, it would be advisable for the modern world to adopt the Stoic outlook and wisdom when it comes to protecting nature.

Ask yourself: when was the last time you saw the kinds of messages that resemble those the Stoic teachers discussed? That we are merely individuals passing by along this journey of life, and that life is short? This is such an oft-mentioned theme within Stoicism, and I believe that if this philosophy had not lost its fame for such a long time, it most definitely would have championed against environmental damage to nature, as in the Stoic worldview, we are mere passersby in this life, and the natural world around us is something to be maintained and looked after. The decline of the Stoics was already underway well before technological advancements commenced, but we can still attempt to take wisdom from them in this regard. For example, we can see from their wisdom that it would not be possible to hold two opposing positions at the same time, so we cannot live in accordance with nature while also prioritising profit and market share at the cost of nature.

"A setback has often cleared the way for greater prosperity. Many things have fallen only to rise to more exalted heights."
—Marcus Aurelius

"Every cloud has a silver lining" is a popular expression known to the masses, and the above quote shows a similar sentiment coming from Marcus Aurelius. Let's attempt to attain wisdom from this, but in the context of this chapter. This kind of success, found by gaining wisdom from failure, will only come to those who have intentionally focused in a specific direction to attain their desires, rather than spreading themselves and their efforts across a multitude of directions simultaneously. By doing so, one can achieve greater heights after many setbacks.

So here, we can determine that we should not be aimless in our pursuit of philosophical knowledge or do so for purely academic endeavours. Attempting to take on positions from all strands of philosophy will only lead to endless reading and thinking. Rather, we should decide to set upon the Stoic path and get what we desire from it to build character, thus attaining new heights of ourselves.

If we consider possible reasons why the Stoic school of thought started losing its popularity, it might be due to people associating this philosophy with the Christian church, as the clergy borrowed from Stoicism as needed. When Enlightenment-era thinking grew in popularity, the roles of the church and state were redefined and people became inclined to draw on other schools of thought than Stoicism, which was seen as offering a similar flavour of thinking as the pre-Enlightenment church. Perhaps these new ways of thinking were more inclined towards pleasure as compared to virtue, as human nature—if not disciplined—leans towards pleasure. If so, this shift in thinking would have been unfair to Stoicism.

Another factor playing a part in the decline of Stoicism is the popularity of Epicureanism, which was the main competing school of thought. Popular modern values, prioritising the pursuit of pleasure, could be seen as an evolved version of the Epicurean school of thought. Some of those who pursue pleasure do so to fill a void within themselves. They are trying to get in touch with their innate dispositions, which are instead perhaps indicating that something else is needed. As the Stoics noted, pleasure is not as enduring as virtue is. One can be satisfied on a level of deeper meaning, which is more long-lasting. Therefore, when arriving at the gates of Stoicism in the modern world, people gravitate towards it, as it provides deeper meanings which are more aligned with their own nature and the nature of the external world.

If the Stoic philosophy were to become part of mainstream thinking, it should be presented to the masses as something to acquire for themselves, as there is virtue within this act. The concept of moderation as a fortress that balances our mental state regarding the material world is particularly relevant in these times of instant fame and riches that young people can acquire without facing adversity. The many who attempt to achieve this instant success miss out on the lessons they could have learnt whilst on the journey of building their character.

Within Stoicism, we also find an emphasis on the importance of service and duty to others, which is something quite secondary in the modern world. Within the Stoic literature, there is no distinction made between "us" and "the other"; rather, the Stoics believed all human beings are deserving of righteousness. Though there are mentions of good and evil people, and positive and negative characteristics, there is no indication that locality should be considered when evaluating people. Within the philosophy, the emphasis is placed primarily on working on the inner self to build a solid foundation, with others as a secondary concern.

So this presents many questions that require more depth for which the modern world is not quite presenting the answers for those who feel such a deficiency is presented to them. Such depth can be found within the Stoic principles. Of course, there will be many people who have already found what they are looking for within all that the modern world presents, which is fair enough. As we know, Stoicism is not part of the mainstream way of thought.

As a reader of this book, you likely find yourself at a crossroads. Two paths lie in front of you. Either you can be content with what the modern world presents, while mixing in a few ideas from the Stoic path, or you can fully take the Stoic path, prepared to face any adversity on this journey and be satisfied with the building of character. Only by facing adversity can one build their character, and the Stoic path is one filled with adversity, in the realms of both the inner and external world.

Let's look at a slightly deeper concept from Stoicism: providence. Modern thought does not offer an alternative to providence, due to an emphasis on a scientific and material view of the worldview. Perhaps we can attribute this to the rise of atheism in the last two hundred years for the most part. We hear such people say they are thankful indeed, but to whom do they direct that thanks? Mother Nature? But what actually is that? They might be thanking a tree or many trees, a forest or a deep jungle, all of which are parts of nature, not the whole, and not the whole of which nature is only a part.

Perhaps I have not articulated all possible aspects of what they might be grateful for, yet the question arises as to whether these very things are even capable of receiving the thanks that are directed to them. Within the context of this chapter, the wisdom we can take from this is that the Stoic path presents a very different path from that which is commonly pursued in modern society. As we traverse along this path, we will face many levels of adversity, as we are products of modern society and therefore we will find many of the beliefs we currently hold will be challenged. This we will face in addition to the general adversity we all face in life. For these very reasons, those upon the Stoic path will certainly face more adversity.

One of the ways in which this challenge can be overcome is through the use of logic, as this can ensure the position we are coming from is one of soundness. Each particular concept in Stoicism will provide us with progress along the Stoic path, although in different ways as these are all interconnected. The Stoics may have foreseen that a time would come when their particular school of thought was no longer popular and that other schools of thought, such as the Epicureans, would be more appealing due to their focus on pleasure. Despite how long Stoicism has been around, it is not as popular as it should be. People are more inclined to embrace vague and loose concepts that encompass many things and are open to interpretation, so anyone can make these concepts suit them. The Stoics have none of this vagueness that can be interpreted in a way to suit society's flavour of the day. Stoicism can be quite rigorous in this regard, which can put off people who are looking to take an easier path. Adopting Stoic ideals can lead to a complete change in character, in a good way, resting on the principles of soundness of reasoning, and enacting such change can be difficult. The way of the Stoics is not something innate to humanity. Instead, it is something that we must train ourselves in and cultivate within ourselves. This can be challenging and may deter some from delving further into Stoic philosophy. However, by focusing on applying Stoic concepts to your own life, you can make what you've learned more relevant to you, and you will see your progress more clearly. No matter what adversity you are facing, the tools the Stoic path provides will enable you to overcome it and gain wisdom from it.

The question then becomes: Why not traverse this path if it is something worthy of pursuing? This path was one trod in ancient times, and though these footprints have long since faded with time, the tools they have left for us will allow us to face any adversity that waits along the path. We can find satisfaction in comparing ourselves to the masses who are not travelling along this path and see we are thinking for ourselves and not mindlessly following the groupthink of society. We may find it a lonely path, yet the adventure of self-growth here can be found. It may get quite dark at times, but we must remember that it is only in the dark that we see the stars.

We can treat the limited Stoic literature we have with us in the present day as an ancient map which is missing some parts. We can still use the parts that are available to us for insight, and we can apply a kind of thought leadership to gain insight into what could have been in those missing parts and lead the way for our individual journey.

"Other people's views can be contagious. Don't sabotage yourself by unwittingly adopting negative, unproductive attitudes through your associations with others."

—Epictetus

We have been considering how one may feel at times along the Stoic path. This statement from Epictetus reveals yet another reason why this path may be a difficult one. What is being noted here is not the dangers presented by the mixing of concepts from competing schools of thought, but from the individuals we come across who carry with them negative mindsets. Epictetus recommends removing ourselves from associating with such people, as these mindsets are contagious. In the modern world, this especially applies to social media, as from behind the safety of a screen, people will find the courage to present far more negative ideas than they would in reality.

When encouraging others to walk the Stoic path, it may be wise to hold off on discussing the second step of looking at the external world. It is important to first make progress in the inner realms before getting into such discourses in the external world. Engaging with others who hold negative mindsets in such an encounter can damage one's confidence rather than encourage them to continue with the Stoic path.

"Today I escaped anxiety. Or no, I discarded it, because it was within me, in my own perceptions—not outside."

—Marcus Aurelius

This statement highlights how the internal and external worlds are interconnected, as it depicts how something from the external world caused something in the inner world. Once this was realised, then Marcus Aurelius discerned what was within his power to control and domesticated it accordingly. Maintaining a positive mindset along the Stoic path is important, but how can we do this if we do not perceive things correctly in the first instance? We can take the wisdom from the above example and apply it to other situations in which emotions present themselves that are caused by something within the external world. We can then separate the cause and the effect within our perceptions, as Marcus Aurelius did regarding anxiety. This is just one of the ways that we can domesticate our emotions as the Stoics did.

As a side note, there are some emotions that are particularly important to acknowledge when they present themselves. These are gut feelings, or some kind of instant emotion that swiftly arrive out of nowhere. Feelings like this should be respected and taken note of, as they may be caused by the subconscious mind making us aware of danger. However, it is important to not let these emotions linger and overshadow our perception of the external world. Instead, we should look upon them as indicators and then put them back in their place, while addressing whatever external factor they were alerting us to. Allowing these emotions to persist and cloud our judgement hinders our ability to deal with the task at hand. Thus, we should domesticate our emotions by dealing with the external cause of that emotion.

We should sharpen our perception and become able to quickly differentiate the kinds of information that we are presented with in order to put things in their proper place. This helps us to order our minds, thus also lessening anxiety by a significant amount. By correctly utilising Stoic concepts, we can keep our minds ordered, and we will find ourselves able to process information as swiftly as it reaches us in this information age.

Most certainly, it is a better approach to deal with things in the moment than to keep putting them off to deal with at a later date. The latter will lead to a build-up of unresolved problems, which will inevitably become burdensome, as we are constantly bombarded with new information in the modern world. Therefore, it would be wise to increase our skills in this regard, so we can effectively apply logic and critical thinking to every situation we are presented with.

We only have a certain amount of time and energy to expend each day, so it's important to be able to see the external world for what it is. By understanding how it is connected to us, others and perhaps nature itself, we can use our rationale to navigate in the desired direction. The importance of the present is often mentioned by the Stoics as it is the only thing one really owns at any given moment. Therefore, it is important to not carry the baggage of unprocessed thoughts with us. There is no logic in keeping any such emotion with us for longer than necessary; otherwise, it can become an obstacle. We'll need to overcome many obstacles along this journey anyway; it would be prudent to not create more of these than there needs to be.

"So you know how things stand. Now forget what they think of you. Be satisfied if you can live the rest of your life, however short, as your nature demands. Focus on that, and don't let anything distract you. You've wandered all over and finally realised that you never found what you were after: How to live. Not in syllogisms, not in money, or fame, or self-indulgence. Nowhere."

—Marcus Aurelius

Many go about life carrying with them a mixed bag of ideas, many of which come from places with contradictory premises. They do not realise that many of the ideas and information that are presented to them do not exist within a vacuum but are rather part of someone else's philosophy or ideology; they simply do not know the source. If we live our lives in such a way, then we have allowed ourselves to become ships with no captain on board to give directions, so we will never find a favourable wind. Thus, we should be the captain of our ship and aim ourselves in a clear direction.

I congratulate those that have made it this far with me on this journey reading this book. By utilising the sound philosophical standpoints of Stoicism to build our characters, we will surely bring about within ourselves some of the qualities and attributes that seem to be getting further and further away from us as time goes on in the modern world. Here, we intend to reverse this trend for ourselves and highlight, understand and develop the aspects of high character, which we all have great potential to possess.

With intent and focus, we can achieve inner fortitude, which is much needed in the modern world for so many reasons. Once this has been achieved, it becomes much easier for us to ignore what others think of us, and still put ourselves at their service if they require assistance towards virtue.

Marcus Aurelius mentions towards the end of the statement that we learn to live "not in syllogisms, not in money, or fame, or self-indulgence". We have discovered that these things do not satisfy us in the sense of having a lasting effect. Yet many have come before and surely many will come after who still follow such desires, so we are advised to be averse to these things and seek to attain something else—that being virtue.

Throughout your Stoic journey, remember to seek wisdom when facing adversity. True wisdom comes well after understanding and practising these Stoic concepts. When faced with adversity that can potentially cause us to falter, the fortitude, resilience and mental toughness we have attained through building our character according to Stoic values will help us to deal with such things. The same mental toughness will ensure you do not falter from the intended path due to external ideas that may not be compatible with Stoicism. In the modern world, we are bombarded with information, and it is therefore essential to acknowledge that you may be confronted with competing ways of thinking. If you are new to the Stoic philosophy, then be aware that you will regularly encounter such things, and ensure you are prepared for when you do.

As the Stoic texts say, personal merit cannot be derived from an external source. We should take courage and apply this concept to ourselves correctly.

Arriving at these conclusions with soundness should not cause worry; rather, we can take courage by knowing we have arrived not by taking the well-trodden path. This path is one that few choose to take for themselves. By looking within and remembering this, we may call upon strength, which is needed especially within the complex and adversarial modern world. This will demonstrate just how much utility can be drawn from traversing this path. We can quickly discern whether ideas originating from competing schools of thought will be of use to us and whether they are in line with Stoic principles. When confronted with a new concept, ask yourself: Does this align with the Stoic principles? Does it not? It is even true? Is it not? Is it popular? Is it not? Does it assist me along my path? Those who do the required work can answer these questions instantly.

These are relatively straightforward questions that can lead to more advanced questions. With this book, all such things could be looked into accordingly. Through examining things from a more advanced perspective, we can ascend to greater levels. With the tools of logic and reason, we should also be equipped to deal with such things correctly and rationally, without being led like a herd of cattle.

There will be times when a simple conversation with someone could steer us out of our character. Keeping the Stoic principles in mind will help to keep us on our path and help to remind us that other people's opinions are external to us, rather than originating from within. This puts our character to the test. Situations such as this can demonstrate to us how far we have come along this path, as it is in these situations that we have the potential to falter.

The Stoics directly challenged the positions of competing schools of thought, and in the modern world we have far more of these than the Stoics ever saw themselves. Seeing how they challenged competing ideas shows us that the appeal of Stoicism could be broadened to reach the majority quite easily. On a basic level, we could say that Stoicism presents us with a more challenging road to traverse than other schools of thought but that it brings about far greater benefits in the long run. The Stoics challenged the majority's inclination towards short-lived pleasures, and highlighted the difference between virtue and pleasure, each being quite the opposite of the other. Virtue is the worthier option to pursue, but it can take courage to do so if we find ourselves at a crossroads between the two. It is part of the human condition to be caught between the two, in whatever varied forms they may present themselves in.

If we conclude that virtue is worthy of its position at the peak of the Stoic path, we are in agreement with the Stoics. As this conclusion is based on more than our individual passions and opinions, we can then make the choice to pursue this path, using the tools we now have within our possession.

You may currently hold beliefs and ideals that originate from the modern world's philosophies and ideologies. Let's bring our attention to how these can be reconciled with the Stoic way of thinking, or dismissed if they are incongruent. Through soundness of reason, you may judge all things accordingly.

In our times, there have been many technological advancements that the Stoics could never have imagined. While it is often fine to embrace technology, as for the most part there is no harm in doing so, there is the risk of technological advancements trying to break established barriers in the fields of ethics, morality, character, conduct towards others and other topics that philosophy deals with. Such pursuits, if unchecked by those that are well-versed with such things—and I cannot think who in the modern world that could be—can lead to outcomes that it may be hard to come back from. However, it is important to note that it may be unwise to adopt the same outlook towards both technological advancements and the philosophical pursuit of breaking ethical and moral barriers, as these fields are quite different by nature.

It can be valuable to examine the worldviews people and nations have held in the recent past through the lens of the insights the Stoics imparted to us. These ideas developed at a rapid pace and gained popularity quickly, having vast consequences for the world, and just as quickly the world realised that these ideas were not good for humanity. Examples of this are more plentiful in the modern world than the ancient world, as the intensity and speed of change have increased. To navigate these changes, it is essential for us to have the kind of fortitude that the Stoics recommended. In this information age, we are presented with many things, some of which are true while some are the furthest thing from the truth. These untested ideas can cause harm and make people falter.

In the modern context, how can we deal with world religions whilst keeping in mind the Stoic philosophy? Here, I will bring our attention to the Stoic concept that it is right "to align ourselves to that which is spiritually superior", as noted by Epictetus. This statement does not need interpretation, as it is written in a clear and direct way by one of the masters of articulation and logic. However, it is worth noting that the Stoics were only familiar with the religious practices from the localities they were from, and there is no evidence in their literature that they ever presented their knowledge in this regard to others from varying religious backgrounds. Perhaps the Stoics arrived at this wisdom because they had the insight to acknowledge that there may be something else out there in the world that they had not yet become aware of.

Readers in the modern world should also strive to align with what is spiritually superior. At some point along their journeys, they will reach a similar crossroads when exploring concepts such as epistemology, ontology and metaphysics are looked into. Seeking alignment with what is spiritually superior may lead one to understand how to apply these concepts in the modern world, potentially taking such a person along the path of seeking wisdom.

Surely, then, we should apply the standards of logic, epistemology, ontology, metaphysics and the other tools that the Stoic path has given us to find this very thing that Epictetus asks us to seek out and align ourselves with. It would not be logical for us to leave behind all such tools and concepts when seeking spiritual truth, thinking they are not relevant. Truly exploring this subject will require all of these concepts, as we seek answers to a number of questions, such as whether a first cause brought all things into existence, as the Stoics believed, or whether their counterparts were correct to believe it was down to randomness and chance. Finding such answers will be a test of the rational mind.

The general Stoic position is that there was a singular first cause. When we find mentions of gods within Stoic literature, it is likely that this was for the purposes of the Stoics engaging with their audience in a way that was familiar to them and to make a stronger point about whatever they were discussing. As an example of Stoic monotheism, when debating with those who believed in chance and randomness, Epictetus described the "craftsman" as the first cause.

In today's world, people often adopt beliefs from a wide range of continuously evolving sources, which can lead to being left behind if one does not keep up with the changes. It is important to understand the direction that our beliefs are taking us. Regardless of our personal preferences, the truth is the truth, and we cannot ignore it due to our personal biases and opinions. Otherwise, once again, we have not seen things as they are and are instead wishing for things to be the way we think they should be.

This brings our attention to yet another aspect of the modern world that should not be overlooked, which is that people who are willing to communicate their various ideas to the masses do so with vested interests. This raises the question of whether what is being presented is actually the truth. Well, it can be, but we should use logic and reason to question and examine these presentations further before taking a stance on their content. We should also be even-minded towards the Stoics and take a similar approach to their messages. We discussed earlier how we can discern the purpose and potential outcomes of following the Stoic path. We should similarly examine the characters of the Stoics themselves and the details of their teachings in order to determine the validity of their message.

Yet another angle to consider when evaluating information is censorship or the threat thereof. In the modern world, we receive information through our phones and laptops from people we do not know personally. How are we to know if the full message is being presented? This censorship seems to be far more prevalent in the modern world than it was in ancient times, especially in mass media. How are we to correctly discern the validity of a message if the sincerity of the individual delivering it can be called into question, or if there is a chance they have been held back from articulating their full message? One should rightly apply the concepts of the Stoics to soundly determine the truth of such situations and deal with them accordingly. It is the task of the wise to avoid such incorrect beliefs that have the potential to hinder our progress towards the places we wish to ascend to.

Often when the news presents a discourse to us, they will bring on people with two opposing positions and give them two minutes each to present their arguments, which is not enough time for them to articulate their points fully. The masses, who are not equipped with the analytical tools of the Stoics, will likely remain with the same opinion and biases that they had before even seeing the debate. There are also instances where one side is represented by an expert in the field while their counterpart is a layperson who struggles to articulate their argument. In such cases, the expert may seem to win the debate, but that does not necessarily mean that they are correct. Only a small percentage of people will have the tools to recognise what has happened and seek out evidence to support an opposing view. This requires using logic, reason and soundness to discern the truth.

As we all traverse this path, we often find ourselves somewhat alone, especially as we delve into the workings of our inner worlds. We should remember not to take two contradictory positions by questioning the foundational ideas of the philosophy which helped us to start and progress our journey. We became aligned with the philosophy only after arriving at it with soundness of reason and by knowing what places we intended to ascend to. Should this be reevaluated as we continue along the path? No. This may lead us to become more like the Sceptics in their methodologies, and the Stoics recommended that one should be averse to this school in particular. We should follow the orthodox route set by this school of thought, as the founders and most prominent members of the school intended it to be.

Thus, whenever two paths open up in front of us, one leading to the Sceptics' worldview in which we will keep on reevaluating the conclusions we have reached and the other one that asks us to keep the outlook that we already reached with sound reasoning, the wise will choose the latter. For if one does as the Sceptics did, then an entirely new school of thought might be arrived at, whether intentionally or not.

For those new to the Stoic path, this chapter has aimed to explore the various elements present in the modern world that may attempt to steer one off the path in some way or another. As I acquired Stoic concepts and tools on my personal journey, these were some of the things that I used those tools to evaluate. Although there may be even more things that you find to put through the rigours of these concepts.

"The highest good is the unyielding nature of a resolute mind, its foresight, its loftiness, its soundness, its freedom, its harmony, its beauty. Do you still require something greater to which these qualities may be attributed?"

—Seneca

There are many ways that "living in accordance with nature" can be interpreted, including the belief that it is referring to living with a rational mind. The quote above is a demonstration of this being referred to as the highest good. In other places, the Stoics make many references to the highest good being virtue. From this, we can see the importance of these two concepts being held in such lofty places.

The pursuit of a resolute mind shall be more readily attainable to those who follow a straight path within the philosophical realms, as opposed to those who mix ideas from various sources to arrive at their own personal philosophy. Mixing Seneca's concept of the highest good with ideas from competing philosophical schools of thought, whatever they may be, would lead to flawed reasoning, as the various aspects would not necessarily support each other. Paradoxes can arise in such thinking, the resolution of which even the soundest of minds will find a challenge. In this case, then, surely the process of ascending from premises to conclusions would have to be different in its entirety and would no longer be Stoicism as we know it today. Fortunately, we still have what the Stoics imparted in its original form, untainted by mixing with other ideas.

We must acknowledge that this most likely is going to be a path that is traversed alone. Many will have a difference of opinion, many will outwardly agree yet hold different positions internally, and some may even actively discourage us. Perhaps this is why the Stoics often spoke of the value of separating oneself from the mob. By reminding ourselves of this concept, we can see that the Stoic teachers were aware their path was more challenging for most individuals to implement when compared to what the other philosophical schools had to offer. Therefore, it was prudent of them to provide such an analogy to illustrate the importance of being able to stand apart from the crowd.

For problem solving, a particularly useful tool is Occam's razor, which is a principle of deduction reasoning that states that "plurality should not be posited without necessity". In other words, precedence is given to simplicity; if presented with two competing theories, the simplest should be preferred.

Through the process of elimination, you can remove all impossible answers to your question until you're left with only one possible answer. We can then take a position upon this answer when it presents itself without being sceptical. I think this is a worthy tool to highlight in this chapter, for it may assist those who find themselves at a crossroads as to whether they should walk the Stoic path alone. However, I shall not complete this deductive reasoning for you, as this is not the aim of this book. I am aware that I have in some manner taken it as far as leading you up to monotheistic religions, with a general path of epistemology and metaphysical uses in these regards, though I imagine people will differ on such positions. Further debate on this topic, though, is outside the scope of this book. These things were mentioned to demonstrate that there is some discussion of such matters within Stoicism, but we must remember that this is a grey area, as the meaning and usage of these terms in Stoic literature is not entirely clear in some places.

The wisdom of Stoicism and its principles are not commonly taught in educational systems, despite the fact that they provide us with tools that we can utilise to deal with life's adversities and overcome them swiftly, enabling us to reach higher ground. As the saying goes: "You have to walk through the mud to get to the higher ground, as there are no shortcuts to get there."

Well, then, another reason to adopt the tools of Stoicism is that we are often conditioned by society and the media to hold beliefs that are not necessarily our own. Additionally, we may hold limiting beliefs that are holding us back for one reason or another. How are we supposed to unpack and unravel such things on our own if we do not possess the tools to do so?

In the modern age, many people need help with mental health issues. We have built tools to help deal with such things, some of which are new inventions, while some are built on ideas taken from ancient philosophies. Many modern tools like counselling and CBT are based on science and do have their practical uses with regard to the solving of issues or perhaps the unblocking of aspects from within ourselves that are holding back our progression. There are many books written on these subjects and academics are continually enhancing and improving these methods.

Comparing ancient Stoic wisdom to modern cognitive therapy, which is better? The modern methods are typically scientific and textbook-like, which can be effective if the person utilising them is motivated. However, they lack the human touch, being quite clinical, and may leave the individual with unanswered questions about the deeper meanings of things. These methods do not exist to explain such things, they are designed to simply address specific issues. That is why the modern methods have these voids within them and why I would suggest that they not only have lost the human touch but that they did not have it in the first place. They do not provide insight into the deeper meanings of things and are not interested in providing the "why" of things but rather the "how". Despite that, these methods are good at doing what they set out to do, and utilising them is far better than simply doing nothing.

Stoicism, on the other hand, provides a more holistic approach. It lays out a path to be travelled and provides the tools to overcome the challenges that lie upon that path. Even if a person did not initially seek to walk the Stoic path, but instead only sought to overcome perhaps one or two specific challenges, the success of the Stoic tools might leave them pondering the questions of what else they can overcome and what other progression can they make. Therefore, it is more valuable to have a set of tools that can be applied to any situation rather than a set of tools only work for a particular problem. This would suggest that a varied toolkit is one that the general public would find easier to understand and utilise.

From my experience, I can say that before I stumbled upon Stoicism, I was struggling with the adversities that were in front of me. Although being very new to Stoicism and not ever being a student of philosophy, I found it resonated with me and I was able to quickly get to grips with the concept of looking within to find strength. I did so whilst learning more from the Stoics. Everything I learned I was able to apply to my own life in real time.

I would even go as far as to say that the Stoic teachings were, for me, easier to utilise than anything I had ever been taught by a motivational speaker or expert. As soon as I discovered Stoicism, it helped me to overcome the challenges I was facing. Looking back and connecting the dots once the adversity was overcome was an insightful experience for me.

This had an empowering effect on me going forward, and I found deeper meanings along the way, and the proclivity towards virtue became much clearer to me. This further highlights that the principles are sound, which we all intrinsically know. Stoicism hands us these concepts as a template to apply to our own lives. I certainly consider myself a student of Stoicism. However, it is important to note that my perspective may be influenced by confirmation bias because of this. Additionally, I have never undertaken any counselling, CBT or any such methods, so I cannot speak from first-hand experience regarding these subjects. While these modern methods do seem to bring some improvement along the way, they do not seem to bring many people to the end of their journeys. Whilst a feeling of ease may be brought about by having a counsellor listen to you, there may not be many long-lasting effects, as such therapy does not focus on providing you with tools to take away with you.

Regarding CBT, this is science-based and covers a vast spectrum of things it can deal with. This kind of therapy is now being suggested by doctors to their patients, and here in the UK is available through the NHS. Therefore, we can see the credibility of such a therapy, as it is very much part of the mainstream methods available to patients. There are benefits to this kind of therapy, although it does have its shortcomings as well. In brief, I believe that if you only have one or two specific issues to resolve, then this kind of therapy could be useful to try. However, if you are suffering from a number of overlapping issues from different timeframes, and this overlap is not addressed or acknowledged by the patient or the therapist, then such therapy will only bring a slight benefit as the underlying causes will still remain, due to this scientific approach primarily focusing on the actual issue only, and not the human condition. There are often plenty of other interlinked issues connected to the actual issue itself. The problems we face can be the result of multiple causes and can be aggravated by even more things. This method therefore does not help the patient to find the deeper meanings of things that they should be aware of, as it does not correct flaws within their logic and rationale. This would leave them with a very superficial kind of betterment from where they started out in the first place.

Stoicism provides a longer road to travel than these modern methods by helping people to better understand their own psychology along the Stoic path, in particular when we are discussing the realms of the inner self.

The concept of looking within yourself to find strength is something that can be interpreted in many ways. However, it should always be a continual practice that becomes part of you. The need for such strength will vary depending on the situation and what issue it is that you are experiencing. This concept can be applied for general purposes or for more specific issues that need to be resolved. This should be combined with the concept of seeing the external world for what it is, which can expose deceptions and allow you to deal with such issues accordingly.

Mastering all the principles within Stoicism will most likely make you truly capable of overcoming any adversity that presents itself from within. As the Stoics noted: once nothing from within can harm us, then we will be able to reach the places where nothing from the external world can harm us.

The Stoics of the ancient times thought of any adversity that presented itself to them as the challenge that they had been training to face when such a thing arrived. While we can take much wisdom from the Stoics regarding how to overcome adversity, we may not actually want to reach a state where absolutely nothing can harm us. However, if these Stoic practices have the potential to take us to such a place, then they will most certainly provide us with effective tools to tackle any challenges we encounter.

With Stoic methods, we can become more astute at seeing, understanding and acting upon both the inner self and the external world without relying on a third party such as a therapist to assist us or anyone else, as with these tools and concepts we become more capable than we once were. This will certainly be more advantageous to us due to the fact that while we may not reveal all the information about ourselves to a therapist, we cannot hide from ourselves when equipped with these tools to avoid self-deception.

"This is not something, however, to which mere surroundings are conducive, unless the mind is at its own disposal, able at will to provide its own seclusion even in crowded moments. On the contrary, the man who spends his time choosing one resort after another in a hunt for peace and quiet, will in every place he visits find something to prevent him from relaxing. The story is told that someone complained to Socrates that travelling abroad had never done him any good and received the reply: What else can you expect, seeing that you always take yourself along with you when you go abroad? What a blessing it would be for some people if they could only lose themselves! As things are these persons are a worry and a burden, a source of demoralisation and anxiety, to their own selves. What good does it do you to go overseas, to move from city to city? If you really want to escape the things that harass you, what you're needing is not to be in a different place but to be a different person."

—Seneca

This excerpt from Seneca's *Letters from a Stoic* provides a good example of how Stoicism deals with a particular situation, and many people can gain insight from the answer given by Socrates here. Many people believe that problem solving is something only done in the external world, rather than within. Though going to different places may provide short-term distraction, the situation they tried to remove themselves from shortly returns, and they will once again be faced with the same adversity that they tried to resolve with short-term methods.

This brings our attention back to how modern methods of self-improvement, even when successful, will often leave you thinking, "Well, what next?" The modern methods do not have those answers. They are designed only to deal with the specific issue that the patient came in to deal with and have no concern for these broader questions or the lifelong journey towards the betterment of the self. This is where Stoicism differs greatly. Stoicism's principles and the pursuit of virtue seek to improve both the inner self and the external world, equipping us with the tools we need to navigate the journey of life. It stands apart from other philosophies, which are merely academic pastimes of those with the free time for such endeavours.

Putting together all we have discussed in this chapter, we can start to form a picture that encompasses some of the adversity that we may face when pursuing the Stoic path. By doing so, we can see the mist clearing in front of us to reveal the path with more clarity. Seek courage from within and set upon the path with only what you can carry with you. While you may share the journey with those others who would seek a similar ascent, this is likely a solitary path.

Stoic Metaphysics

All ancient philosophical schools of thought have their own version of metaphysics. This branch of philosophy often overlaps with epistemology and deals with discovering the cause or causes of things, using sound logic and rationale. It should be mentioned here that the Stoics were master logicians; we can see this demonstrated throughout the Stoic literature. Metaphysics deals with the understanding of reality by using first-principles thinking to look into the first cause: that which created space and time, and all that exists in the universe. Metaphysics also encompasses the understanding of consciousness and being, of mind and matter, of necessity and the non-necessary.

Within metaphysics, predication will be highly utilised to establish correct connections between concepts and premises of consciousness of the mind and matter, along with other concepts. This allows us to see how one premise connects to another premise, all the way through to the conclusion. Metaphysics and the use of predication are interwoven with each other in regard to ascending towards the desired conclusions. Whilst proceeding with these concepts as tools, methods of deduction will also be applied within this process. Ontology will also be utilised, which is yet another branch of philosophy that deals with reality, being, becoming and existence. We can see the usage of this by the Stoics as they often were in pursuit of the correct way to classify things in their correct categories accordingly.

An example of applied metaphysics can be found outside of Stoic literature within the realms of philosophy of religion. One such example is the work of Ibn Sina, otherwise known as Avicenna, who used the contingency argument in his writings, which is quite interesting for those who wish to look into it. I have mentioned his argument in particular as it arrives at a similar position to the Stoics, who refer to the "craftsman", as we have seen noted by Epictetus.

Regarding the workings of the natural world, the Stoics limited their focus to physics alone and did not include biology, chemistry or other branches of science. However, they did include ethics within their usage of metaphysics. In the modern age, metaphysics does allow for the inclusion of more aspects and is not limited to just these elements, but further description of these modern versions of metaphysics and their details are outside the scope of the Stoic school of thought.

Metaphysics inevitably overlaps with logic in many regards, as logic is always a central concept working in the background, essential for arriving at any position with soundness. It is the tool by which the undertaking of the pursuit of metaphysics will for the most part be attained. The Stoics further break down logic into more sub-categories such as language, rhetoric and grammar. These tools are also used in the pursuit of metaphysics.

Our focus shall primarily be on the metaphysics of the Stoics, which can be directly applied towards facing adversity in the modern world rather than purely utilised in academic pursuits. Awareness and understanding of its particulars can broaden the mind towards critical thinking. This concept will assist with this whilst providing a greater understanding of the Stoic way, and its focus on first-principles thinking.

This can lead to better problem solving, understanding of deeper meanings and the ability to reverse engineer things for better understanding. By breaking down concepts back to their premises, all the way back to their cause, we can better understand them. We can also become better equipped to analyse premises to their conclusions.

Such familiarity with metaphysics can enable us to agree or disagree with anything that is presented to us, a skill that is particularly useful in the modern world, where we are constantly and swiftly confronted with new information, such as work and personal emails, current affairs, social media and our relationships. With these tools, we can provide ourselves with a slight edge for our own betterment and that of the external world. This is more relevant in our times than it was in the ancient world, as the constant overload of information can cause a level of stress and anxiety. It is therefore important to do anything that will help us order our minds. As the Stoics noted, the quality of our thoughts is dependent on the quality of our lives. By becoming practitioners of problem-solving in all aspects of our life, we can operate at higher levels and better navigate the demands of the modern world.

"You ask what I seek from virtue? Virtue herself. For she has nothing better, she is herself her own reward. The highest good is the unyielding nature of a resolute mind, its foresight, its loftiness, its soundness, its freedom, its harmony, its beauty. Do you still require something greater to which these qualities may be attributed?"

—Seneca

As we progress, we should not forget that virtue was considered the highest good by the Stoic teachers. In the modern world, there are many distractions pushing and pulling our attention in all directions, and when we take the tools Stoics have imparted to us, we should not leave their ethics, such as virtue, behind. In the above quote from Seneca, we can see an example of the completeness that is the concept of virtue. A similar sentiment can be seen throughout the works of famous Stoics such as Marcus Aurelius and Epictetus. We should note that their works were often not intended for publication but were instead letters, discourses and discussions. This means we do not have records of discourses of concepts from the beginning of the movement, which would show us clearly how metaphysics was used, or a text that outlines this process in a manual or textbook-like form, at least from Marcus Aurelius, Seneca or Epictetus.

The above statement by Seneca presents virtue to us from many different angles, providing a clearer picture of virtue in just a few words. This is just one part of a broader discussion within his works. As we see this concept repeated throughout Stoic literature, we can begin to build up for ourselves a picture of the Stoic metaphysics and the elements of it we have discussed in this chapter, so we can test these concepts for ourselves. In such a way, we can further our knowledge of the Stoic philosophy with the use of their metaphysics. On the other hand, we can utilise the tools the Stoics have provided us with in this branch of philosophy to actually critique some of the ideas discussed in their own letters, discourses and discussions, to see how the Stoic school of thought holds up to being critiqued. This allows us to see if this philosophy can truly be the cliff that the Stoics advised us to be: one that can withstand any onslaught of waves without falling.

The Stoics focused on both material and non-material things in their metaphysics, which covers a vast spectrum of things. While their metaphysics agrees with the positions of Socrates, Plato and Aristotle in some aspects, there are also differences, so it cannot be said that the Stoics agree with these philosophers in their entirety. Modern interpretations of metaphysics have expanded beyond what these thinkers would have considered, and perhaps Aristotle would have disagreed with the inclusion of some of these aspects if he got to review one of these recent books for himself. It is not the intention of this book to delve too deep into the similarities and differences between different interpretations of metaphysics, as such a comparison would start to make this look like a textbook. This has been intentionally avoided in order to widen the audience of the Stoic school of thought, so that there's no risk of you thinking that it's not for you from the get-go if you're not a philosophy student. Some readers may find the old, classical style in which the works of the Stoics are written off-putting. Additionally, they may feel like they have to endure the many aspects of these works which are not of interest to them, as you need to read a complete work in order to find the few gems contained within. That being said, I hope that this attempt to widen the audience for Stoic philosophy will find some success.

As we mentioned earlier, the Stoic philosophers believed that only the educated are free. Therefore, I have included this brief introduction to the concepts of metaphysics and its components so that those towards the start of their Stoic path may start to understand this topic for their own utility should they wish to do so. These concepts can be used to enhance critical thinking skills, which are often missing in the modern world, or at the very least this can be a step towards independent thinking rather than conforming to groupthink, which the Stoics advised against. We have discussed in other chapters the concepts of looking within to understand the workings of our inner world, and metaphysics can also be utilised in such an undertaking.

It is clear that the Stoics compared what the other schools of thought had to offer in regard to what they believed to be the correct direction of ascension, and what the highest good was in their worldview. However, they had built such concepts from the ground up first before making any such comparison. The comparison is a secondary aspect that provides certainty and a holistic analysis. We can see examples of this in the full works of Seneca, Epictetus and the earlier Stoics, where more details are provided.

While there are plenty of statements throughout the Stoic literature on correcting premises and positions of others within discourses, a strict text one can adhere to on epistemology and metaphysics is not available—certainly not the kind of textbook we are used to seeing in the modern world. To get a deeper understanding of these aspects, we shall have to refer to the works of the earlier Stoics for further clarity.

One could say that for the most part, the Stoics were more concerned with the classification of things with regard to the usage of metaphysics rather than the continuous search for new things. Rather than describing the literal meanings of things, they used metaphors extensively. This use of metaphor can be found outside the Stoic school of thought as well. Most famously, the meaning of Plato's *Sophist* is still being debated by scholars today. It is also important to understand how the smaller works in the Stoic school of thought relate to each other and how the subjects they discuss are connected as a whole.

"Let us seek something that is good not merely in outward appearance, something that is solid, balanced, and more beautiful in that part which is more hidden; let this be what we try to unearth. And it is not situated far away: it will be found, you need only know where to stretch out your hand; as it is, we pass by things that are near us, as though we are in darkness, and stumble over the very objects of our desire."
—Seneca

This statement suggests that we need to unearth our sincerity with regard to striving for virtue and not stumbling upon objects of our desire. By stating that we might be in the darkness, it may be referring to how the conditions around us have hindered us from achieving the things that we desire, and we may need to reevaluate them accordingly. We have failed to seek virtue and thus shown a lack of it.

The second part of Seneca's quote suggests that virtue is all around us, and if we pursue it with sincerity, all we have to do is reach out our hand and it will present itself to us, as it actually comes from within us in the first place. Lastly, Seneca reiterates that if we seek pleasure instead of virtue then we are like the one that travels in darkness and stumbles within this darkness rather than attaining the virtue that was a more worthy pursuit.

As there is no formal branch of metaphysics within Stoic literature, we must gain an understanding of their views on the topic through how various concepts are presented throughout their works. There are mentions of how they considered the works of Plato, such as the *Sophist*, but further discussion of this can be left for the academic realms, as such a topic is more scholarly in nature. For those who have chosen the Stoic path with a focus on levelling up their character or building their character, it is simply enough to be able to apply the principles and concepts we have discussed to the frameworks of the modern world.

The Journey Towards Positive Thinking

The Stoics considered positive thinking essential for the progression of their journey. This state of mind is to be sought in particular for the implementation of *amor fati*, which is the acceptance of one's fate, which should itself be done with a positive mindset, as this will improve the quality of our thoughts. These two things go hand in hand as they each bring forth a similar result of blissfulness. The method in which *amor fati* was described by the Stoics was to break down this pursuit into three unique sections: *apatheia*, *ataraxia* and *eudaimonia*. These are set in a linear trajectory; one must attain the first, then the second and then the third.

The step is to achieve the state of mind known as *apatheia*, which despite the name, is not related to apathy, which is a completely different thing. *Apatheia* is a state of mind in which one is free from one's passions.

The passions can be broken down into three further categories, which are *lupe*, *phobos* and *epithumia*. *Lupe* is defined as distress, which is an emotional reaction that presents itself in many forms that can hinder us from the progression towards the path of the above first set of categories that lead to *eudaimonia*, or the highest good. *Phobos*, or fear, can also present itself in many forms, and, if allowed to set in and is not immediately dealt with, then this too can hinder progression towards the desired goals. The third aspect, *epithumia*, or desire, can be a more elusive thing to recognise, especially as it does not cause the same instant negative impact as *lupe* or *phobos*. But it can be just as harmful in deterring the progression towards the attainment of *eudaimonia*. Another difference which further makes this particular concept harder to recognise is that it can present itself in the form of delight, even when it is of a fundamentally more malevolent nature.

It is important to be able to discern between the subcategories of passion to be able to carry out the works of the inner self correctly. It can be easier to identify when something is a thing of lust, but it may not be so clear when it is a thing of delight, due to delight not being associated with being harmful for the most part—though this assumption can be incorrect in many cases. By being aware of these three subcategories, we can see when they have influenced our thinking.

No examples are needed to swiftly move on from these subcategories of passion, which are clearly explained by their definitions. Each person should contemplate by looking within to decide for themselves if any of these are personally relevant issues to be worked on. Through such a contemplation, you may see more clearly the specific obstacles that hinder your personal path. *Lupe*, *phobos* and *epithumia* are to be brought under your control, and not the reverse, as this would surely lead you in quite the opposite direction than that which you set out towards. Familiarity with these concepts allows you to categorise and control them. This then assists with the pursuit of building your character accordingly.

It is within our power to see and understand these passions to get a deeper understanding of what they really are. Then these concepts shall become the tools we can use to either overcome any adversity that presents itself or to clear the mist around an obstacle of a more elusive nature and then overcome it if required. Things that once harassed or hindered our progression can then be replaced by those that assist in our pursuit of the Stoic path.

Let's bring our attention back to the main three concepts that can lead us to peace of mind and positive thinking.

We shall move on to the second of these concepts: *ataraxia*, which is also a mental state. For the most part, this is translated as imperturbability, tranquillity and equanimity. Although there are similarities with *apatheia*, there are nuanced differences which we shall here look into.

Ataraxia is more concerned with living in accordance with nature. Seeking to reform unhealthy passions for healthy passions whilst attaining *ataraxia* by living in accordance with nature will help us to look within and do the work that is needed. This will open the path towards the third of these concepts, and the highest of these mindsets: *eudaimonia*.

Eudaimonia is at the peak of the Stoic mindset. It does not only contain within it simply the state of mind alone but rather the combination of *apatheia*, *ataraxia* and *eudaimonia* for a more proactive approach towards the external world. Once *eudaimonia* is achieved, all three of these concepts are understood correctly and can be applied in ways that will be unique to each individual. Along with all the concepts discussed within this book, these lead towards virtue. *Apatheia* sees us abstaining from vice, *ataraxia* sees us conducting our actions within a wider society morally and ethically, and these concepts and behaviours will eventually see us achieve the state of *eudaimonia*.

Now that we understand the utility of these concepts, let's look at why these concepts should be applied along the Stoic path. Do these concepts tie in with the other teachings we have covered within this book? Simply put, without achieving these mindsets, all we can do is simply follow our passions. Whilst in modern society, this is often viewed as a good thing, the Stoics understood the flaws in this kind of thinking, thus they developed a framework to categorise our passions accordingly and achieve positive thinking. These concepts provide us with the correct tools to make judgements about our daily activities and provide the clarity to see things as they really are.

Achieving *eudaimonia* will bring many benefits in regard to overcoming adversity from the inner self. As a side effect, it may also have a direct effect on our productivity, as we might have freed ourselves in the same manner as the philosophers did. We will not be so affected by obstacles such as overthinking, procrastination, lack of focus and the like, which can prevent us from achieving the results we desire. *Eudaimonia* brings with it all the benefits of positive thinking, as once it is achieved, we are no longer hindered by the moral muddle of our passions. It also brings the potential to achieve high levels of success in our chosen professions or businesses. The combination of these concepts working in harmony creates a perfect environment to maximise results in our work.

Along with all the practices we have discussed in this book, attaining *eudaimonia* can certainly provide us with an advantage towards life and our pursuits. Each of the three stages outlined in this chapter helps us to clarify the direction of the path we wish to take, which in itself creates a certain amount of momentum along the path.

The subcategories of *eudaimonia* we have detailed will assist with a deeper insight into finding any hindrances caused by unhealthy passions. This can be carried out along your Stoic journey, as and when you find such hindrances. This can all be considered part of character-building, which fits in together with many of the broader concepts discussed in this book, which can be used at various levels depending on the situation and circumstances one is presented with.

These mental states that we have just discussed will allow us to highlight and swiftly deal with any obstacles within ourselves that may hinder us from following the Stoic methodology towards virtue and building our character. This allows us to become independent and self-reliant, without the need for any other kind of modern therapy. We can depend on ourselves to overcome any adversity, even that which is within us.

If you were to compare a person who does not possess these tools to one who does, the difference would be quite evident.

As compared to ancient times, we now face more complex and intense challenges that require a rapid response. Therefore, the warrior within us has to navigate a different kind of battle called life and the self. To thrive in this terrain, we need to develop the necessary skill sets.

In modern times, we are confronted with challenging and conflicting ideas from outside our personal pursuits and require a broad knowledge base to deal with. In ancient times, the masters of philosophical schools would challenge different schools of thought. Thus, the audiences present could see these works in motion. This would provide much insight to the workings of these philosophical schools' positions.

In the modern world of competing ideas, only those who have worked correctly to build their character will be able to thrive within such circumstances in a way that is aligned with living in accordance with nature. Those navigating through such times should certainly strive to maintain a positive mental state, which attaining *eudaimonia* will most certainly assist with.

With healthy passions instilled within us, we can think and act accordingly to continue our journey towards attaining virtue—something surely more worthwhile than following whatever is currently popular with society, something that is constantly evolving and has not stood the test of time. The Stoics have advised against becoming like the Sceptics and continually re-evaluating our position. The Stoic school of thought is firmly grounded in the principles that we have discussed throughout the chapters of this book, which are not open to reinterpretation, even in our times. What the Stoics taught then is still relevant to us now.

Once you are familiar with *apatheia, ataraxia* and *eudaimonia,* you can follow the path laid out before us by the Stoics. Each person's path will be unique to them, so you must use these concepts to guide yourself along it. If you ever wonder if you are still on the right path, then you can check your inner world to see things for what they really are. Looking at things correctly will grant you the ability to do the right thing when no one is watching, which brings forth the ability to do the right thing when everyone is watching. This is not the easiest path to take, and you should not embark on this journey without knowing what it involves. At times it can take us to dark places and force us to acknowledge the parts of our character that have not been worked on, whatever they may be. At such moments, we can get stuck. This is why you should take notes throughout your journey to measure your progress. Then, when you face adversity, you can see how you have already applied these ideas and made them part of yourself. It's a good way to motivate yourself and reminds you that you should not be too hard on yourself at these times. You will be able to reset and categorise the adversity you are facing as one of the unhealthy passions and work to replace it with that which is coming from soundness of reasoning.

Epictetus wrote: "On the occasion of every accident that befalls you, remember to turn to yourself and inquire what power you have for turning it to use." This is essentially another way of saying that in the face of adversity, you should look within to find strength. Seneca and Epictetus both articulated the same message in their own ways. We should have the fortitude to inquire how we can turn an external adversity into something that can be of use. The wise will transform these accidents and adversities into advantages.

Some obstacles can be dealt with at the very moment that they first present themselves. We have the ability to stop these adversities head on before they can truly set in and start to take root, thus becoming more of a challenge to deal with. This becomes easier as we get more experience of the various challenges life can present to us, and we develop the tools needed for such an undertaking. We should also be aware of the element of time. It is not always the right time to act. Therefore, mental fortitude is required to wait for the right time, when our emotions are informing us that it is conducive to tackle the adversity. The truly wise will keep their emotions domesticated so that they can instead make any moment the right one by creating the correct emotional conditions.

There is a third type of adversity that we can turn to our advantage, and of the three this can be the most challenging. These adversities arise to prevent the things we pursue from coming to fruition as swiftly as we would like. It can be people we have to deal with who are proving difficult to manoeuvre around. It may be that the economy is not going the way we want. Even these adversities can be turned to our advantage when they present themselves.

These adversities require slightly more strategic thinking to be dealt with, a combination of the techniques we've already mentioned. Fortitude and patience are required, as the discovering and application of strategy is not a quick fix. We should also be prepared that things may not go the way we desire the first time round. There will likely be many small milestones that will need to be achieved before the desired results can come about. The mental toughness, resilience and fortitude required for such things should be fully within our grasp.

However, we should know and recognise the human aspect of ourselves and acknowledge that it may not be so advisable or healthy to have this kind of warlike mindset. So, to endure upon this path, we must use *apatheia, ataraxia* and *eudaimonia*, which will certainly provide us with the positive thinking that will lift our spirits along the way. This allows us to remember the human element—the softness of the heart. Much of the Stoic character-building relies on the idea that nothing external can hurt us. This kind of attitude can potentially harden our hearts to the point where we forget that wherever there is a human being, there is an opportunity for kindness.

The last part of the quote from Epictetus refers to the "power you have for turning it to use". Acknowledging this power within us can empower us to further ourselves on our personal journey. Practising Stoic principles can empower us, and bringing more things within our power makes us stronger. Therefore, this pursuit of power is a noble one.

Some might consider the pursuit of power to be negative and leading to corruption. This is a danger we must be aware of, but we must consider whether those people who find themselves corrupted by the pursuit of power were grounded in the underlying principles of the Stoics. Did they have virtue as their aim? For, surely, there are many examples of those who had power and used it for good purposes as well. For example, the emperors who followed Stoic philosophy chose to take care of what they already had rather than focus on expansion, even though this was in the age of empires. That is why they are referred to as the five good emperors—the most notable of them being Marcus Aurelius himself.

Each person's journey is a unique one, and therefore self-reflection is necessary to ensure that we stay upon the path of virtue. Looking within allows us to see where we may be faltering on any principles and concepts. We can then carry out the works that need to be done to correct our course and re-centre ourselves upon the Stoic path.

Here we can come back to the subcategories of negative passion: *lupe*, *phobos* and *epithumia*, which can be used to address conflicts in the mind. As we start to become more powerful, new issues will arise within us, and these three concepts will again need to be used to analyse and reconfigure these conflicts.

Like with all things, we should be mindful not to side with the extremes on either side of the spectrum. This applies in how we deal with adversity. Depending on the person and the problem, it can be a vice that we need to abstain from completely or simply lessen to some extent. In the modern age we, for the most part, do not have the anchor of a Stoic way of thinking, so we can quite easily fall into pressures or influence of society. Instead of being averse to adversity in the form of negative passions, we may have the proclivity towards it.

By working through the steps of *apatheia*, *ataraxia* and *eudaimonia*, we can guide ourselves towards positive thinking. These mindsets allow us to look within ourselves as needed either to improve our mental state or overcome adversity when things get more challenging. Few other methods of self-discovery and development provide such depth while remaining simple enough for a beginner to understand and work through.

Without utilising the concepts discussed within this book, it is likely that anxiety and depression will persist for those who experience these issues. Of course, modern methods can also be used to resolve such conditions. However, the Stoic school of thought takes a different approach by providing tools rather than solutions. Going through the steps of *apatheia*, *ataraxia* and *eudaimonia* will provide anyone with the potential to seek out and deal with most issues emerging from their inner world. Even for those who are not dealing with such issues, these concepts will prove useful on the Stoic journey.

For those who are not facing such issues within their inner world yet are still looking to learn from the wisdom and well-grounded principles of Stoicism, I would bring your attention back to the chapter title: *The Journey towards Positive Thinking*. In these modern times, positive thinking is needed now more than ever, as the mass media exposes us to things that go wrong in the world far more often than things that inspire us and bring forth the human aspects of us that soften our hearts towards humanity and virtue.

If we dare ourselves to experience the best the world has to offer, then we can become the bigger and better versions of ourselves. The question is, how can Stoicism help us achieve this? While we may not attain the very best, the Stoic journey is in many ways its own reward: the journey itself is the destination. By asking such questions and setting our minds to find the answers, the path will surely open in front of us and our direction will become clear.

***

"Now there are two ways in which a man may be thus hardened: one when his reasoning faculty is petrified, and the other when his moral sense is petrified, and he sets himself deliberately not to assent to manifest arguments, and not to abandon what conflicts with them. Now most of us fear the deadening of the body and would take all possible means to avoid such a calamity, yet we take no heed of the deadening of the mind and the spirit. When the mind itself is in such a state that a man can follow nothing and understand nothing, we do not think he is in a bad condition; yet, if a man's sense of shame and self-respect is deadened, we even go so far as to call him 'a strong man'."

—Epictetus

We should be mindful to not let the hardenings Epictetus speaks of to set into our inner selves. If we notice that such a process has begun then we should immediately work to reverse it, for such a thing can affect us in significant ways which are not for our betterment. It is true today as it was Epictetus' time that if a man's sense of shame and self-respect is deadened, we will view this as a positive trait, although this is an incorrect point of view. Particularly when it comes to celebrities, even if we do not consider them "strong men" for these qualities, we will look upon such qualities as "somewhat OK". What, then, does this say about us? Well, it may be that we too might have become as such. If this is the case, then we can use the concepts within this chapter to deal with this accordingly.

***

To ascend to the heights that we seek, it shall take fortitude, resilience, mental toughness, temperance and positive thinking. It will take courage, it will take self-discipline, and some or all of the concepts discussed in this book. And of course, consistency is a key component for any such concepts to become embodied within us. Consistent practice together with discipline will assist with forming new habits and building our character.

Here, I would like to bring to our attention a subject discussed by Epictetus: "On things in our power and things not in our power." Once we understand what is within our power and what is not, we will be able to re-evaluate our previous thoughts and ideas and realise our biases, which allows us to hold positions with confidence. Once this kind of unshakeable confidence is found, then you can think positively and attain *eudaimonia*.

However, it is important to use caution and discernment when deciding where to place our confidence. An important factor highlighted by Epictetus is our will. For any situation where we must decide whether to approach with caution or confidence, it is our will that ultimately makes this decision. These situations arise from the external world, and thus it is important to remember they do not affect our will, which is not an external thing but comes from within. Thus, we have the power to choose how we respond to external factors.

"What then is the fruit of these judgments? A fruit which must needs to be most noble and most becoming to those who are truly being educated. A mind tranquil and fearless and free. For on these matters you must not trust the multitude, who say 'Only the free may be educated,' but rather the philosophers who say 'Only the educated are free.'
'What do you mean by that?'
I mean this. What else is freedom but power to pass our life as we will?"

—Epictetus

Many of us are slaves to societal pressures, expectations within our relationships, material possessions and other things. Whatever is the case for you, we can use philosophical concepts to free ourselves of these things, should we find ourselves being controlled by them.

In the above quote, Epictetus argues that only those who are educated in philosophy and have understood and applied the concepts of *apatheia*, *ataraxia* and *eudaimonia* are free. Within this chapter, we have seen the details of how this freedom can be attained.

As we proceed along this path, we realise how to deal with the things within our power and also those that are not. This clarity allows us to see further ahead, as the mist clears to reveal the horizon. The importance of our will shall become more apparent, as does how it should be directed according to nature. Each individual who desires to be free of restraints should realise that anything that is controlling them only does so because they gave that thing the power to do so. It is advisable to bring these things under our control rather than let them rule us.

However, there are things that may be good for us to be in a way held down by as they come from a place of truth. These might be things that are in accordance with nature, things that are firmly placed by our rationale, or things that guide us towards virtue. We must discern correctly which things the Stoics truly wanted us to free ourselves from. For surely, they would not advocate us "freeing" ourselves from the very things that we have carried out so much work to attain in the first place. Thus, if we are to be free in the way the Stoics advised, we must understand what this freedom was meant to be. Working through *apatheia*, *ataraxia* and *eudaimonia* frees us from the negative aspects of our passions and allows us the freedom to explore further concepts of Stoicism.

"Material things are indifferent, but how we handle them is not. How then is one to maintain the constant and tranquil mind, and therewith the careful spirit which is not random or hasty?"

—Epictetus

Perhaps the above advice is even more relevant in the present day than it was in the ancient times, as we have around us so many more material things than the ancients did, and this increase in material things necessitates increased interaction with these things.

So then it would be prudent to deal with these things correctly, for if we have the solid principles we have worked on as our guiding light, our thinking about them will become more structured. This makes our task easier, as it becomes easier to keep a constant and tranquil mind. We have educated ourselves as the philosophers did and achieved the very same thing.

With this in mind, any such self-discipline that we strive towards should be grounded in reason, and we should understand the reasoning behind it. This structured thought process will inevitably bring forth the resilience and mental fortitude necessary to maintain positive thinking and stay on the path, even in the face of adversity. Though it is common knowledge that this is a good thing, many struggle with maintaining such a mindset. To assist with this, we can look into Stoic thinking and see which concepts will be prudent to take and utilise within our modern context.

Emotion can easily stir within us and cloud our judgement. Even if you ultimately get through a situation where you allowed yourself to be influenced by emotion, you could have dealt with it better and achieved a better result if instead you had utilised logic and reason. For example, if you work in sales and a customer is rude to you, it is easy to absorb some of that emotion and become rude yourself. In such a situation, it would be wise to take a step back, breathe, let go of that absorbed emotion and then move to the next customer. Otherwise, you will carry the absorbed emotion to the next customer, which will not bring the best result, as the next customer will pick up on this and try to distance themselves from you. So take a breath and a small moment to quickly re-evaluate your emotional state before you make that next call, write that email or speak to any stakeholder.

This temperance you demonstrate will speak for itself, and you can proceed to do the right thing.

Temperance is a quality valued by Stoic thinkers, so seeking to increase this quality is a worthy cause. However, this can require work, as situations and people in the external world are likely to test the quality of this characteristic. You must forget all your excuses and do what must be done every single time to maintain this state of being in the face of adversity.

"For my part, I will be indifferent to fortune, whether she flows towards me or ebbs away. For my part, I shall view all lands as my own, and my own belongings to others, thanking nature on this account."

—Seneca

The above statement is part of a longer discourse, and this part in particular can be interpreted in many ways. Although inserted here for how it relates to our focus on positive thinking, you can also see this as a good example of temperance—a subject we have discussed in another chapter. We should not fall into the common misconception that the Stoics were completely divorced from having material possessions. By looking at this statement, you can see the focus on the mindset by which Seneca discerns the reality of the material things within his possession.

The Stoic mindset is one of fortitude. You must accept that there is no loss so great that one cannot start again. The mentions in the above quote of land and belongings are not to be taken so literally but are instead emblematic of this idea. Lastly, we can see in this quote gratefulness, which provides satisfaction—though to whom this is to be directed is a big subject. Seneca thanks nature, yet in the modern world, nature, as vast as it is, is just part of a greater whole, and perhaps even this whole has something greater beyond it, which we may find if we were to attempt to go beyond where Seneca did in this regard.

We can take insight from how the Stoics speak of nations. We can see here how Seneca has affirmed that he shall see all nations as his own. We have also seen that his counterpart Marcus Aurelius considered "nowhere" to be the same as everywhere in the world. But how shall we take insight from this apparent contradiction?

I would argue that there is in fact no contradiction here. The two thinkers are presenting two different ways of looking at the external world, but both are leading to the same outlook. For "nowhere" can mean literally "everywhere", and if we connect both these statements together, we can see that both mention how all is within nature, which they are living in accordance with.

"Whoever has joined the ranks of virtue, has given proof of an honorable nature: the man who pursues pleasure is seen to be enervated, broken, no longer a true man, likely to descend into shameful practices, unless someone helps him distinguish between pleasures, so that he knows which of them reside within the bounds of natural desire."

—Seneca

Bringing together the concepts discussed within this chapter, we see that *apatheia*, *ataraxia* and *eudaimonia* provide a method of ordering one's mind and the inner self correctly, in pursuit of positive thinking. This can then be connected with temperance, endurance and virtue, which together act as a secure foundation to further one's journey along the Stoic path.

Whenever the path branches ahead of us into the path of virtue and the path of pleasure, it is the task of the wise to choose virtue. For pleasure will only cause one to descend, yet virtue will assist in the ascent to achieving lasting effects that will strengthen our character, the way we sought at the start of this journey. Working towards virtue helps us break free from societal norms and align once again with our innate dispositions. Once again, we shall clear the mist in front of us to further gain clarity of the external world, thus realigning the realm of the inner self back to the disposition we just discussed, and continue our journey ahead.

Discourses Towards Ascent

"You are able always to have a favourable tide if you are able to take a right path."

—Marcus Aurelius

In both the professional and personal worlds, many of our interactions with other people include some sort of negotiation, however subtle this may be.

What are the Stoic ideas we can apply to such situations to help us always find a favourable tide and take the right path? While the specifics will be different in each negotiation, there are some things that will be applicable to all scenarios. Most certainly, you should always try to direct the conversation towards whatever conclusion you set out to achieve from the outset, regardless of any resistance or obstacles you encounter. The more seasoned negotiator will be more in tune with how to overcome such things. You should determine the fastest and most efficient way to obtain your chosen objective, which often involves taking the most direct route. Another applicable principle is the idea of looking at things and knowing them for what they truly are, as this will help you to see through any manipulative tactics utilised by the other party. You should also contemplate the situation before entering such a negotiation; you should be aware of what both sides' positions are and what they have to lose and gain. With all this in mind, you should also remember to keep yourself directed towards the aim throughout the process.

Adaptability is an important skill in negotiation, and it can be learned with experience. It is important to keep an open mind with wider horizons in sight and challenge yourself to ensure you work outside your comfort zones. By challenging yourself in such a way, you will be able to adapt to more situations with greater ease than someone who prefers to keep within their comfort zone. You will know how to improvise better with the tools you possess to meet your chosen objective. By combining adaptability and open-mindedness, you will be able to overcome any situation by creating a favourable tide for yourself.

"The first rule is to keep an untroubled spirit. The second is to look things in the face and know what they are."

—Marcus Aurelius

You will encounter both astute negotiators and some less experienced. Either way, you should maintain an untroubled spirit, which can provide the clarity needed to take the advantage and avoid being taken advantage of. For long-lasting relationships, it is important to create a space in which both parties can gain and achieve a win-win situation. Taking this approach is in line with the principle of virtue. By communicating this position clearly to your counterpart, it is likely that they will work towards a similar goal. Be honest and forthcoming with relevant information, and you will win your counterpart's trust. Such an approach will lead to actual benefits.

"Every hour focus on your mind attentively... On the performance of the task at hand, with dignity, human sympathy, benevolence, and freedom."

—Marcus Aurelius

A sharp mind is one of the most important tools you can possess in a negotiation. As highlighted by Marcus

Aurelius, every hour you should focus on your mind to gain inner strength and sharpen your most valuable tool. Justice, ethics and self-respect should be maintained within any negotiation. It is crucial to include human empathy in your thinking, as companies often only think of their stakeholders or a specific subsection of people, while overlooking others. Therefore, you should adopt a holistic perspective in your decision making and consider the possible impact such decisions may have on everyone as well as the environment and nature. Benevolence should always be a guiding principle, and it will most likely lead to good outcomes. If you have the freedom to operate within the marketplace, then you will be able to bring strength and growth to your organisation. If you consider all the mentioned aspects in your decision making, then most certainly your strategy will be successful.

All these factors should be continually running through your mind throughout the negotiation process. This will guarantee a smooth process each time, and, in the long term, will put you at an advantage, as you will have won your counterparts' trust. After a few interactions and experiences have led to productive and good outcomes, they will help to make the process easier.

Most people think that negotiation is a topic mostly related to sales and business. While it is used in such situations, there is a broader array of matters that require similar thinking and skills. Taking the same approach in such situations will inevitably lead to more beneficial outcomes.

Stoic thinking can bring many advantages to any negotiator. When your counterpart is trying to move you towards their own position, the Stoic will keep in mind the immovable mountain that you can be in these moments. On the other hand, when you are trying to move the negotiation in a particular direction, you can flow like water, moving around any obstacle in your way. What gives us the ability to be either of these is looking at the situation in the face and seeing it for what it is. This gives us the understanding needed to use our wisdom correctly.

No Task Is Too Small
or Too Big So Lead From the Front

"Do not act unwillingly nor selfishly nor without self-examination, nor with divergent motives. Let no affectation veneer your thinking. Be neither a busy talker nor a busybody."

—Marcus Aurelius

Many a business leader will have started their career by doing menial tasks. As organisations grow, more admin tasks are created for all those involved. As the saying goes: "a true leader leads from the front." Therefore, it is recommended that every once in a while, you should get into the trenches to lead from the front and by example. This approach will motivate lower-ranking team members, who will then have more respect for you and will be more open to being led. This will, in turn, help you by clearing any veneer from your thinking.

Self-examination, as recommended in the above quote by Marcus Aurelius, reveals different kinds of adversity that we may be facing from our inner selves. By acknowledging these challenges, we can keep our minds sharp and find a tactical approach to overcome challenges.

Those at a similar level to yourself within the organisation may consider such a leadership style to be something which is not the norm or beneath your position. However, you have adopted the mindset of the Stoic, and in doing so, you are seeking to see the world as it truly is. Since the world is ever-changing, leading any organisation towards success will require the robustness to steer it with method and logic in the right strategic direction. For this to be achieved in real time, you must have the foresight to navigate past any obstacles encountered along the way.

Success can be a lonely road, particularly when others fail to understand your vision, but as the saying goes, those who fly alone have the strongest wings. Let us, then, have the strongest wings. In business, no task is too small or too big; everything is important, and everything must be done right and delivered to clients at a professional and high-quality level, exceeding any service offered by your competition. It is essential to always keep your competition in mind, as they are always looking for any given opportunity to outperform your organisation.

In today's competitive marketplace, even the slightest drop in quality or service levels below clients' expectations can quite easily lead to losing a client. As the saying goes, you are only as good as your last job. Most businesses pay much attention to the acquisition of new clients and the growth of the business. However, once these new clients are acquired, they may end up being serviced by more junior teams. Relatively small errors can frustrate these clients, and such errors often go unnoticed by the senior teams, leaving them unable to do anything to repair the relationship with the clients. By leaving our managerial posts once in a while and getting in the trenches, so to speak, we can attain a real-time insight into the challenges faced by junior teams, which will be of much benefit to the organisation.

"Be like the headland on which the waves continually break, but it stands firm and about it boiling waters sink to sleep."
—Marcus Aurelius

Do not allow other people's opinions to divert you from your path. Keep on going and be unshaken by what is said about you. However, do make some allowance, as some things that are said can be of relevance to you. The only thing that you should let move you is your own judgement of these external factors. If you believe anything is possible, then that will be true for you. You decide how it is that you will react; you do not have to react the way it is expected of you. Remember the above quote: you are the headland, and other people are just waves. The waves will come and go, but you will remain. At the same time, do not forget your wisdom and rationality, and always seek self-improvement. Regardless of the challenges others may bring, you should remain constant in challenging yourself to live the life you want to live and pursuing your goals, whilst all the while advancing on the path to virtue.

Regarding the analogy of being the headland, it is important to develop yourself to withstand the pressures that come from people and situations whilst maintaining an even mind. Logic, reason, philosophy and rationality will be the drivers to cultivate the even-mindedness that was sought by the Stoics. Ultimately, you should only act when your judgement tells you it is the right time for you to do so.

"As you start to walk on the way, the way appears."

—Rumi

Early on my path, I listened to a lot of motivational speakers and self-development material, and at times I still do. Much of this can be very useful, but it can be challenging to navigate through the many methods discussed and understand how to apply them specifically to the actual organisation that you are trying to build. Many people struggle with this and do not progress because they do not apply what they have been taught correctly. They may find motivation, but it only lasts for perhaps a few moments. It is important to note that every organisation is unique and not all strategies will be suited to every organisation. As we progress on our journey, we will learn many lessons that we will need to put into action. The key is to find and learn them fast enough, which will make all the difference in not slowing us down to the point where we consider giving up.

If we look at seasoned entrepreneurs, we can see that their success does not depend on whether their current venture is related to their first venture or if it is something they have experience in. It only matters that the idea is good and the people executing it are good. In my journey, I have found that making progress really does depend on hard work. There is no escaping this; success is a step-by-step process. As you work hard and gain experience, you will get smarter. You will start to work smarter and harder, utilising your newfound skills. Keep repeating this process, and you will get better and better until you become a master. Then you must decide to become the student again. However, this time you will start smarter. By instilling all these methods within your teams, they too can benefit and achieve greater success.

In my early days of business ventures, I was once in a business which I had built from scratch to some success. However, after a certain point in time, I had a realisation after reading Sun Tzu's *The Art of War*. The quote in particular that resonated was "Know the heavens and know the earth and you will surely succeed." In a military sense, Sun Tzu meant the weather and the terrain. I converted this wisdom to a business context and asked myself the question: "Do I know anyone who has succeeded and gained as much success as I want to in this industry?" Unfortunately, the answer was no. I was in a business in an industry that was quite easy to enter—maybe that was why I was in it in the first place. "Would I be better off in another terrain? Maybe

I am standing in the wrong landscape at present." Again, the answer was not favourable, as I had already implemented a number of tactical strategies that were more than enough to stabilise the business towards growth. I would be better off spending the same amount of time and energy in a different business in another industry, which would bring much more progress. I was torn between pushing further or changing course, and I applied sound reasoning to make the decision. If you find yourself in such a position, it is advisable to consult with others who have greater experience than you in these matters, after you've considered the situation to the best of your ability.

When making such a decision, you'll find factors such as emotions quickly come to the fore due to your attachment to something you started and grew to a significant level. Everything you have built thus far is on the line based on this decision. What I did was stop all marketing efforts, and I offered the existing team my clients, which they were quite happy with. In such a situation, it may be that the mind and heart are against each other. Well, as the saying goes, from every failure comes a greater success. If you do decide, with reflection, that such a situation will be counted as a failure then so be it. Such a decision has to be made correctly for the greater good and the good of yourself, and it has to be done ethically so that the least harm is actualised for anyone involved.

This is part of leading from the front. After any such event, you should not think of it as a loss, but as part of a process of acquiring greater wisdom and skills, leaving your next venture more likely to succeed. You can look within to find much strength which, along with your experience, can now be harnessed towards a new path.

"How simple to reject and to wipe away disturbing or alien imagination, and straightaway to be in perfect calm."

—Marcus Aurelius

Certain kinds of thoughts must be cleared away to achieve perfect calm. This calmness is what brings about the clarity we need, most specifically in difficult situations. This will be needed by those who operate in high-pressure, fast-paced work environments. Some of us may, to some extent, do this already. Some may do so quite automatically and intuitively, perhaps because they are used to these environments. Though, quotations like the one above can serve as a reminder that this perfect calm can be attained more regularly.

This brings our attention to the subject matter at hand, that being how to improve our reality from within and how to improve the external world by harnessing the ability of the mind to excel in all the tests that the external world throws at us, thus being able to make our dreams a reality, thought by thought. This journey makes us feel great from within along the way.

To lead from the front, as we have been discussing, is something of value. Why should this not be applied to the internal self as well? With a determined mindset to push forward on the right path, no matter the cost, we can attain higher levels of self-improvement. Then how can we do this? It will take burning the midnight oil and putting in the work, but anything is possible. In adversity, you will find your true potential and build the character required to achieve something truly extraordinary.

By understanding what is within our control and what is not, we can keep an untroubled spirit, as we know that we can improve that which is within our control, and that which is not should not be the cause of any worry. This mindset will help us focus correctly on that which should be focused on.

It can be challenging to motivate team members who feel content at their current stage. Unlike larger organisations, small organisations do not have the luxury of having team members that are not continuously improving. So, how do we encourage our team members to challenge themselves and improve? There are many ways to approach this, and the most effective will vary from one organisation to another. However, it is essential to continually approach this topic, as it is for the greater good of serving others. If your team members internalise this, it will benefit the whole organisation.

"A stoic is someone who transforms fear into prudence, pain into transformation, mistakes into intuition, and desire into undertaking."
—Nassim Nicholas Talib

The above statement highlights that Stoicism is not just about accepting things as they are, but rather, seeing things as they are and changing them for the better. The betterment will be for the internal self and the external world. This particular statement, however, is referring to the internal self. The first thing mentioned is fear, something which all people feel at some point and can relate to. Here it is suggested to turn fear into prudence by using discipline to govern oneself with reason. Similarly, pain can be transformed into any number of things that will serve us better than the pain itself, and mistakes can become intuition as we gain experience and move forward into new situations equipped with what we learned from past mistakes. Desire can be turned into an undertaking by focusing on a particular goal and taking action towards achieving it. This last point, the transformation of desire into undertaking, is a noteworthy aspect of Stoicism that distinguishes it from other philosophical schools. Stoicism is not just an academic pastime but rather a practical philosophy that can be applied to daily life. This is shown by the fact that an undertaking is something one sets out to achieve.

The difficulty of different challenges varies from person to person and also depends on whether something is a small step or a bigger one, and whether it is related to the inner self or the external world. The key is to keep moving forward whilst striving for improvement. This improvement should draw on all the concepts discussed throughout this book. Leading from the front is actually an undertaking in itself, and we must treat it this way in order to do it effectively, treating the actual objectives we seek to obtain as a separate matter, though still connected.

The Strengths From Within
Always Should Be Seen

"If a man knows not to which port he sails, no wind is favourable."
—Seneca

The ability to navigate through life while being fully in the present, neither held back by memories of the past nor worries about the future, is a skill like any other; it requires practice to become better. The intention of this chapter is to help you come to a better understanding of how to navigate through life so that you may be in a better position to be present in the moment, to operate with a clear lens and not one skewed by your biases and expectations.

Truly looking within yourself to find your greatest capabilities is not the easiest task to undertake. It requires sharp focus on a daily basis, discipline and awareness. It is not going to happen immediately and requires consistent effort. As with any undertaking, we can look to teachers and books to advance us to a certain point, but once this level has been reached, we must personally discover the subtle nuances that will help us ascend towards true mastery.

"Look well within thyself; There is a source of strength which will always spring up if though wilt always look."
—Marcus Aurelius

The Stoics always looked within to gain strength and find their true potential. It does not matter what others think and say; it only matters what you think. Be an independent thinker. While most birds fly in groups, you should have the awareness to be the eagle that flies alone at a much higher altitude. From such heights, you can see much further.

Quite often, people will reach a particular level and then lose sight of the fact that there is another level to reach after this. Maybe life takes over, or maybe the challenges they once faced have been overcome, and now this level has become a comfort zone. Such a comfort zone can be welcome for a short while. You should take a well-deserved break to take some time to reflect upon what it took for you to overcome these challenges and how you were able to build your character to reach this point. It's also an opportunity to use foresight and wisdom to consider what you may face further along the path. Unfortunately, many people become complacent and remain within these comfort zones, forgetting the goal of their entire journey, and that there is still much further to go along the path. It can be very easy to stay within the status quo. Only with constant self-reflection can you keep progressing towards the next level and achieving your true potential.

There can be trials and tribulations that happened in the past that hold us back. It could be something someone said. It could be something that happened. It could be the loss of someone. There are many such things within our memory that could be hindering our progression. How would a Stoic deal with such a personal matter?

Healing from the past can be a long process, and it can be helped by quieting down the mind in a safe place without distractions. Focus on going through, working out and coming to terms with any such thoughts with humility and reason, regarding that which happened and regarding oneself. This will help to lighten some aspects of these hindrances and allow for further progress. To fully live within the present, one must not let the distractions of the past and future weigh them down. We should aspire to have a mind that's free, steadfast and fearless. As the saying goes, you should empty your mind. Make it formless, shapeless, like water, which can take any shape to fit its current condition. In this state, the answers will come to you with greater ease.

The mind is a powerful tool, and asking the right questions will lead to receiving the right answers.

A good basis to start will be to draw upon one's own knowledge and wisdom attained from personal experience, but it's important to derive the correct wisdom from these experiences. Choosing a philosophy such as Stoicism can help provide a solid framework for gaining deeper insights, and leading a more substantial and virtuous life. While it may take time to develop the mind and reach these levels of wisdom, once this is achieved, it will lead to a more organised and less complicated journey through life. This is because we will have learned how to correctly deal with our emotions and not let them lead us by default.

Stoicism can assist us in reevaluating our values, thus providing direction for us to follow for the pursuit of excellence and building character within ourselves. It is important to seek guidance and direction to find a deeper meaning before one sets off on life's journey, something mostly missing in modern educational systems. Stoic thinking can assist us in becoming adventurers, as while we all have our unique, personal path through life, all those who embrace this philosophy will direct themselves towards the development of character and virtue.

In the modern age, we are taught that pleasure and individualism are of the utmost importance. However, the ancient teachings of Stoicism show us that self-control and serving others can be of greater importance. We should look within to find strength, allowing us to take the steps as advised by the Stoics for the greater good. This is of higher importance to personal growth than a focus solely on material possessions and competing with one another for these possessions. While this is a game of much allure, it is also one of much illusion.

The illusory nature of the external world is a teaching found in many different philosophies and belief systems. I recall a verse from the Quran: "O son of Adam surely if we were to give you two valleys of gold, surely you would want a third." This is quite a simple statement that anyone can ponder on. Anyone who does so will come to the same conclusion that it is true. One must ponder such a thing with an open heart and reason to discern the truth. Anyone can attempt to provide a counter-answer to any statement, but will this rest well with your intellect and provide peace from within? In the modern world, most people hold opinions that were not originally conceived by themselves. Many argue in favour of matters they do not even believe to be true, and that contradict other beliefs they hold. Maybe they are paid to do so; maybe they choose to misguide themselves and others. Certainly, these are confusing times. This may be why some teachings of old, like Stoicism, seem refreshing and resonate with people such as myself.

The Stoics also believed in fully living life in the present and making sound judgements based on the present moment. They recognised that if we carry the past on our backs like a heavy backpack, it will most definitely slow down our progression towards all things we pursue, and especially the peak we wish to reach, which is virtue. We should instead harness our past experiences that provided us with knowledge and wisdom in order to give us strength to push forward along our path. If some of our troubles persist after attempting the suggestions within this chapter, then one can participate in voluntary hardship to further reveal the things one takes for granted. As noted by some Stoics: wear the scantiest fare and then say to oneself, "Is this what I was fearing most?"

It is important to acknowledge that some parts of the past and present are very much able to hurt and break us. However, since each person's experience of life is unique, this philosophy can be interpreted in a unique way to suit each person and better their progression. What we must do is build ourselves up from the places that tore us down. We can use these as lessons, and rather than let these experiences hold us down, we should turn them into wisdom that becomes the force that drives us onward. Use this newfound wisdom to become a force for good and steer yourself towards virtue, as kindness is better than conquest. You do not know what you are capable of, so find your potential and be kind to yourself, as you can work through that which has been holding you back. Once you have put in the work, you will find the peace that you sought. Take note that it is choice not chance that shapes one's destiny.

"The first rule is to keep an untroubled spirit. The second is to look things in the face and know them for what they really are."
—Marcus Aurelius

You will be better placed to seek insight from this statement once much work has been carried out from within. Once you are on an even playing field, not being held back by the past, you will be free to walk in any direction you wish, as many paths will open as the mist clears in front of you. You will find it easier to look ahead and see things as they are.

Should you take the path of safety, a well-worn path with many signposts? Or a path untravelled, which you will be the first to walk? Why not assume leadership of yourself and take the less-travelled path? If you are the first to walk this path, going forward there will be no right or wrong answers. There is only more learning along the way. There is adventure to be found on this journey if you look at it this way. As you make progress, you will find some critics along the way. Let them speak, as their words only matter to you if you let them. They cannot see the nuances of your experience from your perspective; they can only speak from their standpoint. Your perspective is the only one that counts. Always remember this, and take strength from it.

Perspective is important, as things may appear quite different from a different angle. How, then, do we know whether our perspective and understanding of a thing is correct and holistic? An even mind will be able to make the necessary adjustments needed to correct one's perspective accordingly. Adopting an attitude of understanding based on reason can also allow room to add more rationality to our original impressions and remove our personal biases. A certain level of humility is required to make the adjustments needed to do this.

By working on one's inner strengths, a certain level of calmness will be achieved and an even mind fostered. Be a traveller that can handle all types of terrain and conditions; keep with you all the tools that can give you the advantage to scale new heights and see views more beautiful and virtuous.

Bringing our attention to the practicalities of leading an organisation, you should look within to find your strength and consistently look towards progressing to greater heights. It is equally important to encourage the people within our organisations to do the same. An organisation is made up of individuals, each with their own strengths and weaknesses. Although some of them will be actively working on themselves already, others will not be doing so. As a leader in a position of responsibility, you can promote ethics and share your philosophy, as within most organisations, the culture flows from the top down.

The culture of any organisation simply comes from a group of people holding similar beliefs and attitudes towards the company they work for. Creating and maintaining the desired culture requires careful attention. It may be helpful to have at least one team member who fully understands your outlook. You can then task such people with bringing forth the desired company culture.

Businesspeople often need to get used to handling pressure. This should be quite normal for those who were involved in a company from its start-up stage. At the start, there may not have been much pressure as there was not much business, but as the business grew, those involved from the beginning would have had to train themselves to handle pressure. Another way to look at this is to say the current level of the business growth correlates with the ability of those involved to handle pressure, as different complicating factors arise at different points in a business's development.

More importantly, your primary focus should be on working on yourself. By all means, do spend some time working on your weaknesses, but it should not be nearly as much time as you spend on your strengths. No matter how much you work on your weaknesses, there will be others who will run circles around you in these areas, as these things are, in turn, their strengths. It is better to build a team that has strengths that are not your strengths. The synergy of such a team with a varied set of skills will better serve the organisation and help it to thrive in the business landscape.

Once you understand your strengths, work daily with excellence to take your organisation forward. Lead from the front, and along the way help your team to also become their best selves. By adopting this approach, the entire team will start to work in coherence with each other and become a force to be reckoned with.

It takes courage to make that call to get new business. It takes courage to face a client and let them know your guys did not get it quite right. It takes courage to present your ideas to potential clients. Therefore, it is beneficial to create a company culture that facilitates and enables the entire team to go out and make things happen without the fear of making mistakes.

By creating a culture of self-discipline as well, the team will take responsibility for their own work. This is better than creating a culture of fear, where team members are constantly in fear of being disciplined by the senior team if they make mistakes. To successfully create such a culture, it is important that everyone has an understanding of its importance and that some initiatives are in place to promote and reinforce it. It is also essential to initially recruit individuals who are already aligned with this culture and to create a team with this attitude. By doing so, half the work of establishing and maintaining the desired culture is already done, allowing you to focus more on yourself. Remember that personal development is of primary importance, and the organisation is secondary.

The Stoics believed in looking within to find strength, then looking things in the face to see them for what they are. Once you have found the focus and desire of what you were seeking within, you may look to the external world and correctly judge the scenario, circumstances and people. When this is done, you may bring about this new strength from within to the external world and use it to make changes to the external world in alignment with nature and your ethics.

Once in a while, you should invite team members to strategic meetings who would not usually be invited to attend. They are often the ones really on the ground, and they will have insights into what the organisation needs that you may have overlooked. Seeking their counsel and then acting accordingly is a wise decision that can benefit the organisation. This can expand your own wisdom and understanding, by allowing you to gain insights from different perspectives. As noted by philosophers, you must be able to walk with kings without losing touch with your roots.

There is a saying from Prophet Mohammed (PBUH): "Speak the truth even if it is against yourself." The above statement aligns with the nature of justice and represents a peak of understanding of the subject. The pursuit of true justice requires the willingness to hold oneself accountable. Justice is a central theme within the Quran, and in my exploration of Stoicism, I have found a noticeable similarity between the two, despite one being a religion and the other a philosophy.

The concept of "looking within" can have a deeper meaning beyond self-reflection. It can also involve the pursuit of knowledge and understanding in things such as logic, reason, epistemology, metaphysics, philosophy and spirituality. These tools can certainly assist in advancing any undertaking. However, it is also important to remember that over time, we should develop knowledge and experience in the pursuit of our desired goals.

By executing the ideas discussed within this chapter so far, you will be able to enhance both your inner and external worlds. Now, we will focus on the mental fortitude required for virtue, both for yourself and the organisation that you serve. By incorporating projects that benefit local communities and charitable causes, you can set your organisation towards both success and virtue. An ethical organisation has a feel-good factor about it, and you can lead the way for this with your team, as you have subtly spread Stoic values across your organisation and within its goals. This will make it easier for you to focus on yourself, which is of the greatest importance as it provides you with more of a chance to follow Epictetus' advice: "Don't explain your philosophy, embody it."

One should aim to become a beacon of civility, leading by example in the fast-paced, information-overload world in which we pursue our business goals. It is also important to reinforce the desired company culture by reviewing it with all stakeholders and making it clear to them what heights they can achieve together when working in accordance with the organisation's ethics.

You may encounter resistance from your team on this front. If you do, remember that you are coming at this from a perspective of a higher level of philosophical ethics. If you can communicate this to them in a way that is easy to understand, it will save much time and avoid long, drawn-out conversations. These are the times when you will need to demonstrate your knowledge of Stoicism and be the master and teacher. Throughout this book, we have mentioned that it is best to approach Stoicism with the mindset of the student, as this will not stagnate our learning. However, sometimes you must switch hats for a short time to suit the situation in front of you.

You want to fix the problem, not just win an argument. You are trying to take your organisation up the rungs of the ladder of Stoic thinking, so consult and also take counsel from your team to achieve this. Do not lose your way in doing so, and reevaluate and use your wisdom and judgement to monitor the progress of your team over time.

"Associate with people who are likely to improve you. Welcome those who are capable of improving. The process is a mutual one: Men learn as they teach."

—Seneca

As noted here by Seneca, when you are looking for candidates for new positions in your organisation, you should look for individuals who are likely to fit the culture you are trying to create. Keeping this in mind will leave you and your organisation in a better position to pursue the Stoic path. Otherwise, it is likely that disrupters will end up joining the organisation, potentially causing cultural shifts that are not aligned with your philosophy.

To effectively align all stakeholders with a Stoic outlook and ensure all team members are pursuing the interests of the stakeholders, it is essential to communicate with others with thought leadership, expressing your ideas effectively in a way that many can comprehend.

"We should every night call ourselves to account: What infirmity have I mastered today? What passions opposed? What temptation resisted? What virtue acquired? Our vices will abate themselves if they are brought every day to the shrift."

—Seneca

Although the Stoics aimed to make obsolete the need for social validation, which can cause much distraction and divert us from our goals, modern life places a great focus on social media and validation from others. People seek such validation for the upkeep of their emotional states.

Between stimulus and response there is a space, and within that space, we have the power to choose our response, and in our response lies our potential for growth and freedom. Use this space wisely to adjust your emotional state and act accordingly with a clear mind. This is aligned with the Stoic concept of making yourself an immovable mountain. Additionally, honing one's listening skills can be an essential part of seeing things as they truly are, as they allow you to properly address your counterpart's points in intense discussions, and ensure that both sides can come to a more satisfactory resolution.

All of the concepts we have discussed will contribute to bringing about a critical ability that many people lack: the ability to confront any obstacle, whether it originates from within or an external source. This chapter has so far focused on both the betterment of the internal self and the external world in the context of a business organisation, as well as some relevant ideas and philosophies.

As noted by the legendary boxing trainer Cus D'Amato: "When you get hit, that's when you've got to be calm." The problem is that you may have been hit and have not realised this; in such an instance, you may as well be the sheep led by a shepherd. This is not in agreement with Stoic thinking and its emphasis on self-realisation and not giving value to social validation.

After making progress in these endeavours, you should check whether in the depths of your internal self, you have a dark side. What does this mean? Some sports professionals have explained this aspect of the internal self, which can be a dark and destructive quality that some people can tap into. Most people will not be able to see this part of themselves. For some, when they see a small part of it, they may run away from it. Some will lock it up, knowing the damage it can do.

For example, there is an interview with Mike Tyson in which he describes this dark side as a character that he is no more. Sometimes he misses this part of himself, as it is the person he used to be. Without him, in his words, he feels like a scared little boy. But if he calls upon this dark side, then all hell is coming with him, as the destructive aspects of this character would not stay confined within the ring and spread to his entire life. Keep in mind these statements are coming from someone we regard a legend in the boxing world, who is to this day one of the most talked about boxers of all time.

In this example, Tyson recognises the real-life damage this innate quality of his inner self can bring with it. If we look back further, we can see that when he was a kid, he was always getting in trouble with the law. We can assume this quality was always with him. Maybe it was his environment that brought out this quality quite early on, but that is another subject.

At a very young age, he was scouted by Cus D'Amato, the legendary trainer of champions and friend to Mohammed

Ali. D'Amato let Tyson stay at his house and train with him in the sport of boxing. The first thing he did was get his psychology in order by containing his dark side and then directing it accordingly to the purpose of becoming a champion.

To add further to this, we can also take note of Tyson's psychology when walking up to the ring for a fight. He says that he felt fear. He imagined his opponent beating him. He dreamed of his opponent beating him. But once inside the ring, he felt like he was unbeatable. Perhaps this was a technique used as, due to the nature of the sport, the possibility of losing and the fear factor are experienced most strongly when walking to the ring. Then once this line was crossed, all these possibilities of failure and emotions of fear and embarrassment vanished, and Tyson brought forth the objective he had trained for. At that point, nothing else mattered but winning the fight.

Unfortunately, as D'Amato passed away and other influences entered Tyson's life, Tyson was no longer able to contain and direct his dark side as he had been taught to do. After much turbulence, years later, he gave the interview mentioned above, giving us these insights. To become the world's youngest undisputed heavyweight champion is something truly remarkable. From his story, we can take the wisdom that one might be trained to their highest ability by one of the best trainers in their field, but ultimately at some point, the journey continues without the master. At such a point, we will have to remember the solid foundations on which our craft was taught to us and fully embody what the master taught us, so that we may still progress to new heights.

The question is then whether we have a dark side within us, and if so, how can we correctly utilise it?

If you have looked within and found you do not have such an aspect to yourself, this should not be taken as a negative. All of the remaining details discussed within this chapter are relevant to one's attainment of virtue, which is of most importance. However, if you are aware that this quality exists within you, then we can discuss this briefly.

Another small example I can mention here is Kobe Bryant, who mentioned going to GOAT Mountain, which is a metaphorical place that existed in his mind. In this place, he spoke with all the basketball greats of past and present to discuss the details, strategy and tactics needed to win his next game. In some interviews, Kobe discussed his dark side and explained what this meant. He spoke of having within him many dark feelings such as rage and anger, and thinking that if he is going down, he is going down his way. In doing so, he took these dark emotions—some more examples of which are resentment, frustration and sadness—and transformed them to use as a weapon, at the same time motivating the whole team to do the same. We can see the results of this, as Kobe is remembered as one of the greats in the sport.

Psychology, resilience and mental toughness can all be fuelled by this kind of dark side. Another factor in controlling it will be practice and preparedness, as mentioned by Tim Grover in the book *Relentless*.

From the two examples above, we can get some understanding of what the dark side can mean, from two of the greats in two different sports that require completely different skills. The question arises: can this dark side be of use in any other endeavour?

I would argue that it can be, if it can be realised in the first place. However, it is definitely not something to bring to the fore unless you have the ability to keep it under control and direct it towards good and your pursuits without letting its destructive side cross over to other aspects of life where it does not belong.

"To yourself as well as to many others it is plain that you fall far short of philosophy. And so you are tainted, and it is no longer easy for you to acquire the reputation of a philosopher. Your calling, too, in life has a rival claim. Therefore, if you have truly seen where the matter at issue lies, put away the question of what men will think of you and be satisfied if you live the rest of your life, be it more or less, as your nature wills. Consider accordingly what it does will, and let nothing besides distract you; for experience has taught you in how many paths you strayed and nowhere found the good life: not in logical arguments, not in riches, not in glory, not in self-indulgence, nowhere. Where then is it to be found? In doing what man's nature requires."

—Marcus Aurelius

To get a better understanding of looking within to find strength and insight, we should consider our attention span. Who do you think will have a better understanding of a subject: someone who spent two minutes studying it, or someone who spent two hours? The problem is that in the modern age, people are getting used to receiving information in very short formats, often less than a minute, which in turn makes them accustomed to deriving their knowledge from this type of information. Just as we should instead give due respect and take time to understand external subjects, we should do the same when looking within ourselves to find strength and insight.

How else could we fully contemplate statements from philosophers that pose thought-provoking questions, and derive deep meanings? By investing the correct amount of time in these matters, the answers will present themselves. Although our minds may present us with a good few answers in the moment of reading such a question, we should not stop there and be content with those automatic responses. Those who take a few more moments to explore the deeper meaning of the concepts presented will be in a stronger position. The same principle can be applied when looking within to find strength and insight about oneself. By investing the necessary time and effort, one can achieve greater results and be able to look their inner world in the face and see it for what it truly is.

Exploring your inner world can be a journey of self-discovery for those who seek to know more about themselves. The thoughts and questions of philosophers can guide you on such a journey. Among various schools of thought, Stoicism stands out in this regard due to its focus on development of character and virtue. Virtue is considered the ultimate goal of the Stoics, but when was the last time any of us heard the word "virtue" used in the media? I certainly cannot recall hearing it even once as something of any substance that made me think, "Right, let me look into that."

It is wise to write our thoughts down as they come, so we can think through them later. Another good practice is to read more from great thinkers, starting with as little as 15 minutes a day. Watching debates online can also enrich your understanding of the two conflicting views being presented, which may increase your understanding of your own positions. These practices assist us on the path of discovery of one's nature, as mentioned in the earlier quotation from Marcus Aurelius.

Individualism, happiness and pleasure are key themes in today's philosophy. The philosophy of the ancients, on the other hand, focused on a collective society. We can perhaps take inspiration from both of these, in that we should better ourselves and then serve our communities, transferring our focus from happiness and pleasure to service and virtue, in regard to both ourselves and the external world.

Many philosophies and ideologies in the modern world are competing with each other, not to mention the left and right wings within the political sphere. The media can quite overtly or subtly present these competing messages to the public. If you are not aware that any such messages are from a broader ideology, then you may uncritically accept such ideas. This is not to say that these ideas are inherently bad, but they should be understood in their fullness, so you can make your own decision as to whether you subscribe to them.

The ideas of the Stoics are built on solid foundations. Once we have a better understanding of this philosophy, we can use it as a yardstick to then measure any other modern philosophies and ideals that we come across. Furthermore, once you begin the pursuit of building your character, you will be better placed with greater rationality than you were before any such undertaking. A better understanding of yourself and the external world has been sought and walked towards, with the aim of virtue.

"No soul is willing to be robbed of truth, he says. The same holds of justice, too, of temperance, of kindness and the like. It is most necessary to remember this continually, for thus you will be more gentle to all men."

—Marcus Aurelius

Bibliography

Al-Ghazali. *The Incoherence of the Philosophers.* Translated and annotated by Michael E. Marmura. Provo: Brigham Young University Press, 2000.

Epictetus. *The Discourses of Epictetus and the Enchiridion.* Vancouver: Royal Classics, 2020.

Grover, Tim S. *Relentless: From Good to Great to Unstoppable.* New York: Simon & Schuster, 2014.

Ibn Sina, *Ibn Sina's Remarks and Admonitions: Physics and Metaphysics.* Translated and annotated by Shams Inati. University Press, 2014.

Marcus Aurelius. *Meditations.* London: Everyman's Library, 1992.

Mushashi, Miyamoto. *The Book of Five Rings.* Translated by Stephen F. Kaufman. North Clarendon, VT: Tuttle Publishing, 2004.

Seneca. *Anger, Mercy, Revenge.* Translated by Robert A. Kaster and Martha C. Nussbaum. Chicago: University of Chicago Press, 2012.

Seneca. *Dialogues and Essays.* Translated by John Davie. Oxford: Oxford University Press, 2008.

Seneca. *Letters from a Stoic.* Translated by Robin Campbell. London: Penguin, 2004.

Seneca. *On the Happy Life.* Translated by Aubrey Stewart. Independently published, 2017.

Seneca. *On the Shortness of Life*. Translated by Aubrey Stewart. Independently published, 2022.

Seneca. *On the Tranquility of the Mind*. Translated by Aubrey Stewart. Independently published, 2022.

Sun Tzu. *The Art of War*. Translated by Stephen F. Kaufman. North Clarendon, VT: Tuttle Publishing, 2021.

Xenophon. *Conversations of Socrates*. Translated by Hugh Tredennick and Robin Waterfield. London: Penguin, 1990.

Author Profile

Born and raised in London, Rahail Khan has worked on a number of business ventures in the sectors of BPO services, property maintenance and technology. He has always been interested in self-development, with a focus on helping others develop to reach their goals.

While going through some difficult times in which he found himself lacking the answers needed to overcome some of life's challenges, he by chance found the Stoic philosophy. Coming from an Islamic background, the Stoic way of thinking instantly resonated with Rahail. With this newfound wisdom, the turbulence passed, and he achieved a new form of personal growth.

One quote from the Stoics is "If you want to be a writer then write." Following that advice, Rahail is here to share the wisdom of the Stoics with you.

Rahail can often be found hiking and taking in the beauty of nature—literally living in accordance with nature. Or perhaps he'll be at the gym, doing all sorts of cardio and weights. He has a keen interest in the art of boxing in the peek-a-boo style, used most notably by Mike Tyson, who was taught it by the late Cus D'Amato.

Rahail is offering a select number of readers free mentoring for a limited time to provide deeper insights into the concepts discussed in this book. For more information, please email: info@stoicascent.com

For a wealth of resources, please visit www.stoicascent.com, where you'll find a blog and weekly newsletter that cover many aspects of Stoicism. This will include many things that other modern writers have yet to cover, and is a place of insight for those who are looking to advance along the Stoic path.

What Did You Think of *Stoic Ascent?*

A big thank you for purchasing this book. It means a lot that you chose this book specifically from such a wide range on offer. I do hope you enjoyed it.

Book reviews are incredibly important for an author. All feedback helps them improve their writing for future projects and for developing this edition. If you are able to spare a few minutes to post a review on Amazon, that would be much appreciated, and you will also be assisting others in starting their journey towards living in accordance with nature.

rowanvale books

Publisher Information

Rowanvale Books provides publishing services to independent authors, writers and poets all over the globe. We deliver a personal, honest and efficient service that allows authors to see their work published, while remaining in control of the process and retaining their creativity. By making publishing services available to authors in a cost-effective and ethical way, we at Rowanvale Books hope to ensure that the local, national and international community benefits from a steady stream of good quality literature.

For more information about us, our authors or our publications, please get in touch.

www.rowanvalebooks.com
info@rowanvalebooks.com

Printed in Great Britain
by Amazon

33300711R00128